Religion and Empire

FACETS

Selected Titles in the Facets Series

Religion and Empire

People, Power, and the Life of the Spirit

Richard A. Horsley

Fortress Press
Minneapolis

RELIGION AND EMPIRE
People, Power, and the Life of the Spirit

Cover image: Bart Michiels/nønstock. Used by permission.
Cover and book design: Joseph P. Bonyata

ISBN: 0-8006-3631-7

Manufactured in the U.S.A.
07   06   05   04   03   1   2   3   4   5   6   7   8   9   10

Contents

PART THREE
Religion of Empire

Acknowledgments

This book is the result of a decision by the leadership of the New England Region of the American Academy of Religion and the Society of Biblical Literature, particularly Linda Barnes, Joan Martin, and Christopher Matthews, to make "Religion and Imperialism" the theme of the spring 2000 meeting. Subsequent events—the attack on the World Trade Towers and the Pentagon on September 11, 2001, and the aggressive United States government's response in its "preemptive strike" invasion of Iraq in 2003—have shown how prescient they were about the need in biblical, theological, and religious studies to address issues of imperial power relations. When colleagues I had suggested were unable to deliver a plenary address to the meeting, I was "tapped." The research and ruminations behind the presentation, including the six focal case studies, were an attempt to engage conversations among the various subfields and specialties represented in the American Academy of Religion and the Society of Biblical Literature: Buddhism, Islam, Judaism, history of religions, ancient Near

Eastern religion, theology, ethics, and philosophy of religion. As a specialist in biblical studies who had pressed for attention to the ancient imperial context of biblical texts, I was delighted to find that specialists on religion in India, China, and South Africa were already investigating imperial power relations as key factors in religious formations. We can surely benefit from each others' explorations. I lean heavily on some of them in this survey of case studies.

After making the presentation in the spring of 2000, I researched the cases and issues more fully. The result was an unwieldy "paper" of nearly a hundred pages in draft. A drastically condensed version, completed before 9/11, was included in a selection of papers from the meeting published in *Journal of the American Academy of Religion* in March 2003. I am grateful to *JAAR* and its editor-in-chief, Glenn Yocum, for allowing phrases and paragraphs that appeared in that article to reappear in this book. The 9/11 attacks and the U.S. invasion of Iraq in the face of intense domestic and international protest created a different context for my research and reflection on the relations between religion and imperialism. Serious attention to issues of religion and imperialism is increasingly urgent.

I must express deep appreciation to many colleague and student friends who have had an important hand in the research, reflection, and writing that have gone into this book. Rebekah

Gerstein, Gabriel Gottlieb, Marlyn Miller, Alice Phoenix, Audrey Pitts, and Maureen Worth researched the various subjects covered. Winston Langley guided me into the difficulties of understanding modern Iran and Shiite Islam. Kwok Pui-lan led me into important recent work on Buddhism and in postcolonial criticism, and presented a most suggestive and helpful critical response to the delivery of the original paper at the spring 2000 meeting. Kathleen Sands gave extremely helpful criticism and suggestions in responding to successive versions of the paper, particularly in theorizing religion. Ran Huntsberry offered invaluable suggestions on shaping the presentation of materials and making the argument intelligible. Finally, I am most grateful to the dedicated and patiently helpful staff at Fortress Press, particularly K. C. Hanson for suggesting that a long, unwieldy paper might be shaped into a Facets book, and Ann Delgehausen for many clarifications in the presentation.

Introduction

The terrorist attacks on the World Trade Center and the Pentagon on September 11, 2001, brought the realities of international power relations crashing into the prevailing domestic tranquility in the United States. If one focuses on the symbolism of the targets it is clear that the attacks were not against America so much as against the global forces of transnational conglomerates headquartered in and symbolized by the World Trade Center and the military enforcers of the "new world order" headquartered in the Pentagon. Nevertheless, these tragic attacks indicated that a number of people in the Middle East had become angry and frustrated to such an extreme that they could plan and execute such devastating terror. Why? How?

It quickly became evident that a combination of three interrelated factors motivated the attackers. They were angry at the western capitalist consumerism that has invaded their lives and undermined their traditional values. They were frustrated by a political powerlessness to resist repressive regimes backed by the United

States. And in reaction they had become intensely dedicated to a renewed Islamic faith.

Americans, however, including most academic experts on international politics and religion, were unprepared for these events. There was a considerable gulf between Americans' understanding of the world and the realities of the world. Historians, political scientists, and Middle East specialists tended to exclude religion and religious movements from their study and analysis of political-economic affairs. Even theologians and scholars of religion tended not to consider political-economic affairs as relevant to religion, which they understood primarily in terms of personal belief and morality. After all, the United States and other western countries—where most academic specialists live—had long since established a "separation of church and state," a separation of religion from politics and economics, of cultural expressions from concrete power relations.

Thus not only were Americans and others utterly unprepared for the realities of "political Islam," they were oblivious to how both capitalist expansion and marketing practices and U.S. political policies had become key factors in generating Islamic revival. Seizing the opportunity created by the "war on terrorism," the neoconservative strategists now prominent in the U.S. administration are arguing that America has indeed become an imperial power, the new Rome, and ought to wield its power aggressively against those who would oppose it. Yet many Americans still prefer not to think of themselves as an imperial superpower. They identify with their country's origins as God's New Israel, attempting to build a society of "liberty and justice for all," under the guidance of divine providence. That may be why many were surprised also by the intensity of American patriotism unleashed in response to the attacks on 9/11, a patriotism that makes many people willing to sacrifice their rights for a greater feeling of security. The collective expression of Americanism, with the ubiquitous American flags and "God Bless America" signs on every other house and automobile, was a sudden reminder of the importance of American civil religion. The highly diverse and seemingly atomized American populace suddenly appeared to be mobilized in support of the exercise of the overwhelming U.S. power in the world.

These deeply unsettling events pose concrete challenges to the ways in which religion has been understood and, indeed, constructed in modern western societies as quite separate from political-economic power relations. They pose a special challenge to those of us engaged in the various subfields of religious, theological, and biblical studies. The place from which most western academics view the world is the imperial metropolis. The fields of religious, theological, and biblical studies have grown up as cultural products of the same European powers that established empires over other peoples of the world. We have been socialized into the discourse of established fields of inquiry and interpretation.[1] Our views of and attitudes toward Eastern peoples and religions, such as Arabs and Islam, for example, are strongly influenced by deeply rooted stereotypes that were developed by travel literature and novels as well as by the foreign service and academic studies—the discourse called "Orientalism."

Religious studies has been very much like the field of English literature in this regard. The imperial power relations involved in the very setting, plot, and characters of canonical texts have seemed unimportant until recently. Indeed, political-economic relations in general have been ignored, seen as irrelevant to the aesthetics, cultural content, and ideas to be mined from our special texts. The most important task before us may be to consider how religious practices are related to the imperial power relations that have determined people's lives for centuries, but have gone unnoticed and unanalyzed. By no means are all religious practices determined by their relation to empire. Yet it is surprising how much of what we study and teach is closely connected with imperial power relations.

Since we are only beginning to raise questions about religion and imperialism in religious studies, it seems premature to attempt any comprehensive theoretical overview. Perhaps the most we can do in this short book is to raise some theoretical issues in connection with

some representative cases of three particular
patterns of relations between imperial power
and religion: (1) cultural elites in the dominant
society, no longer satisfied with their own traditional religion or seeking solutions to their
own spiritual malaise, construct subject people's religion for their own purposes; (2) peoples subjected to foreign imperial rule mount
serious resistance by renewing their own traditional way of life; and (3) those situated at the
apex of imperial power relations develop an
imperial religion that expresses and eventually
constitutes those imperial power relations.

In this book we can examine six representative cases—one ancient and one modern example of each pattern. Each example illustrates
how, in various ways, imperial relations determine not only political-economic life but also
the conditions and possibilities of cultural identity and religious expression. In selecting the
cases and framing the discussion, I have attempted to engage conversations among various subfields and specialties in religious
studies, such as Buddhism, Islam, history of religions, ancient Near Eastern religion, Judaism,
theology, and philosophy of religion. In particular, the modern western construction of "classical" Buddhism is analogous to ancient Roman
devotion to the Egyptian goddess Isis. Similarly, the revival of Islam in Iran in response to
western modernization is analogous to the ancient Judeans' insistence on their own traditional way of life and adamant resistance to

Hellenistic-Roman imperialism. Also, the constitution of imperial power relations by the Roman emperor cult is highly analogous to how the ostensibly "secular" imperial religion of consumer capitalism has incorporated Christmas as its primary festival.

Before examining representative cases, I should pause briefly to describe at the outset what I mean by *empire* and explain why it is problematic to define the term *religion. Empire* is commonly used with reference to a dominant nation or regime's control of the territory, people, or resources of another country. It is often thought to begin with military conquest and to proceed by colonization, indirect rule through client regimes, or alliance with the aristocracies or oligarchies of subject peoples. Some imperial powers or regimes also impose their culture on subject peoples or suppress indigenous cultures so their cultural imperialism compounds the effects of their political-economic imperialism. The Babylonian and Persian empires of the ancient Near East, for example, ruled through local rulers and maintained local tributary religious political-economies as an instrument of imperial rule. The western empires of Alexander the Great's successors and the Romans ruled through some local regimes, such as the Temple State and Herodian kings in Judea, but generally advocated or imposed western cultural as well as political-economic forms on the peoples they conquered.

The modern western empires of of the Spanish, French, and British involved far more colonization of the vast areas of the world they conquered—such as India and the Middle East—than had ancient empires. They also aggressively imposed European culture and Christianity. Although most Americans may not think of the United States as an imperial power, it picked up where the Spanish, French, and British left off almost as soon as it gained independence. The "farsighted" author of the Declaration of Independence, Thomas Jefferson, "purchased" most of the vast territory west of the Mississippi from the French, but not its indigenous inhabitants. In their westward expansion, European Americans exterminated the Native American peoples or herded them onto reservations. The United States took control of both the land and the people of the Southwest from Mexico by military force.

From the mid-twentieth century, by virtue of its economic power and military supremacy, the United States moved from one of two superpowers to the sole remaining superpower. Although U.S. military forces are stationed at many points throughout the world and are moved quickly anywhere to suppress any disruption in the "new world order" of the *pax Americana*, the United States dominates mainly through client regimes and "international" economic institutions such as the World Bank and the International Monetary Fund.

Some analysts argue that the real imperial superpower is now the decentralized but complex and intricate network of global capitalism, with the United States military serving as its enforcer. Whether it be the United States, with its powerful economy and global reach, or the global capitalism that is centered in the U.S., empire now exerts unprecedented economic power worldwide and imposes western, mainly American, culture through the highly sophisticated and irresistible modes of electronic media.

It is problematic, however, even to try to define and illustrate *religion* because the term, as understood in western academic discourse as well as popular usage, is so peculiar to modern western society. Indeed, the way *religion* has been understood is one of the principal reasons we now are realizing that we do not have a very good grasp of how to understand it in integral relation with or even embedded with other aspects of life. Each of the six cases discussed below poses certain key issues that seriously problematize the way that religion is understood in western religious and biblical studies. Most significant among these, surely, is the modern western reduction of religion to individual belief. Closely related is the separation of religion and political-economic affairs into different realms of life, institutionalized in western societies as the separation of church and state. That separation has been widened recently by the serious marginalization of religion in social-economic life.

The separation of religion and politics, moreover, is ideologically grounded in a dogmatic insistence that religion be excluded from affairs that belong to the secular realm, which (ironically) is so sacrosanct that it remains beyond criticism. The intent of the separation of church and state, of course, was not to exclude religious influence on the political process, such as calls for more humanitarian state practices, but mainly to prevent the political establishment of a particular church. Yet religion that presses a social-political program as inseparable from its religious doctrine and thus threatens to encroach on the secular-political is labeled as "fundamentalism," while concrete power relations remained unexamined. The net effect of all these factors is that religious and biblical studies tend to separate religion from power, obscure the interrelationship of religion and power, and even mystify the effects of power.

PART ONE

Religion Constructed by Imperial Elites

While membership declines in mainline Christian churches, more and more Americans seek spirituality in sweat lodges and serenity in Eastern modes of meditation. College and university religion departments offer courses on Buddhism, Hinduism, Taoism, and Sufism. Until recently, however, little attention has been given to the origin and construction of what is being studied in such courses or practiced on spiritual retreats. If the manufacture and marketing of religion were regulated in the same way as those of clothing, then many of the "Eastern" religions current in the United States would have to carry labels that indicated that they were "made in America." Part of the aura and attraction of these religions, however, is their origin in the hoary antiquity and wisdom of the East or among peoples who were closer to the earth.

Thus it is not surprising that until recently little attention has been given to the imperial power relations involved in the construction of "Eastern" religions. It is becoming evident that cultural elites in countries that dominate peoples have adapted subject people's religion for their own purposes. The American appropriation of "Tibetan" Buddhism provides an instructive case. But that is merely a continuation of what began in the heyday of western European imperialism, and recent critical studies of western construction and consumption of Buddhism alerts us to a similar phenomenon under the Roman Empire, where Roman elites eagerly sought initiation into the mysteries of the Egyptian goddess Isis.

1.

"Classical" and "Tibetan" Buddhism

While lecturing in the United States in 1894–95, the British scholar Thomas William Rhys Davids made a telling statement regarding a significant phenomenon of European imperialism:

> It took its rise among an advancing and conquering people full of pride in their colour and their race, in their achievements and their progress. . . . It made its first conquests in a great continent occupied by peoples of various races and holding widely different views. . . . And it soon spread over the frontiers among the nations, some of them more barbarous still than the then most uncultured Indians.[1]

This could be about the Spanish, French, or British conquest of America, or the British military in India. But it is about Buddhism—or rather about the "classical" or "pure" Buddhism constructed by Davids and other western intellectuals during the previous half-century.

"Early" Buddhism was presumed to be a product of the vitality of classical Indian civilization, a vitality that had long since vanished in India and had lately manifested itself in nineteenth-century Europe.[2] In recent hindsight, however, this "original" or "pure" Buddhism can be recognized as the product of the Oriental Renaissance in Europe, with its fantasies of lost wisdom, its search for the languages of Eden, and its construction of classical ages long past, coupled with denigration of contemporary "Orientals."

Sensing a missing element in European civilization, European Romantics sought their own lack in the East. French intellectuals of the Enlightenment had idealized China, its teeming population ruled by a class of gentlemen-scholars (the mandarins). German Romantics focused, rather, on India as the abode of the spirit. "Everything, yes everything without exception has its origin in India," proclaimed Friedrich Schlegel.[3] By mid-century, however, both China and India had been demoted in favor of Greece—classical humanism had its origins in Europe after all. After the Opium War of 1839 and the Indian Mutiny of 1857, China and India were considered corrupt and decadent civilizations, the people incapable of governing themselves, thus justifying European conquest and colonization. Nevertheless, a fascination with Indian civilization persisted into the late Victorian period in two ways in particular. Some Europeans identified with the

Aryans, a fair-skinned race of conquerors in the Indian subcontinent whose exploits were now being repeated by their European descendants. Others were attracted by the Indian philosophy of reason and restraint: "classical" Buddhism.[4]

This "original" Buddhism, as constructed by Europeans—with certain input by their elite "Oriental" informants—had certain distinguishing characteristics. First, it was derived exclusively from texts. European diplomats and scholars traveling or stationed in India searched for manuscripts, which they expected to lead them to the lost wisdom contained in "classical" Buddhist texts. Translation and understanding of the texts they received, however, involved an ambivalent relation of both trust and suspicion of "native" Buddhists. Western scholars hesitated to trust the authority of native scholars, yet they could not read the texts without their help. They treated the native informants therefore merely as supplementary to the text whose answers must be checked against the original, access to which, ironically, was provided initially by the natives. Once the texts had been gathered and the languages deciphered, however, the native interpreters were superfluous.[5]

Second, for discovering "original" Buddhism, therefore, real Buddhists in Asia were of limited, mainly instrumental importance. Not only did the classical source supersede the vernacular, but the manuscript superseded the informant. This, of course, was a dramatic contrast with actual Asian practice, which consists of a symbiotic relationship between monks and lay people. In fact, without this monk–lay person relationship there could be no Buddhist practice.

> The role of the monk is to maintain a certain purity . . . [that] renders the monk as a suitable "field of merit" to whom lay people can make offerings, thereby accumulating the favorable karma that will result in a happy rebirth in the next life. . . . In return, monks receive the fruits of the labor of the laity. . . . Monks do what lay people cannot do because they generally do not know how: recite texts, perform rituals, and sometimes meditate.[6]

Third, "classical" Buddhism consisted primarily of the philosophy that had been produced by a small circle of monastic elites and become inscribed in texts. It eventually included meditation, as well. Here was a religious alternative to western religion, or perhaps rather here was what western intellectuals wanted religion to be: an agnostic, rationalist, ethical individualism grounded in philosophical reflection. As we now know, in Asian practice, this special knowledge was only for a certain minority of monks who had gone through many years, even decades, of discipline and training. The denial of an enduring self to an individual was not seen as relevant to the lives of lay people. Despite its absence or even repudiation among Asian Buddhists (as noted already early in the nineteenth century), the teaching of no-abiding-self proved most attractive to western intellectuals.[7]

Fourth, this "original' Buddhism did not include ritual. Now we know, of course, that Buddhist practice in Asian societies involved a great deal of ritual. Ironically, the first Buddhist texts given to Europeans were ritual texts for the ordination of monks, thus indicating that whoever gave them these texts thought that ritual was key for understanding the Buddha's message (somehow lost in "translation"). The very capacity for knowledge depended on ritual preparation, which in Theravada Buddhist communities generally presupposed ordination.[8]

With its reduction to classic texts and avoidance of both practicing monks and a rich ritual life, the western construction of Buddhism seems particularly affected by a Protestant Christian model of religion. And the narrow emphasis on knowledge bespeaks a European Enlightenment reduction of religion to personal belief. In all of these ways it seems clear also that "Buddhism" has been "represented in the western imagination in a manner that reflects specifically western concerns, interests, and agendas," as those are both embedded in and work their effects in modern imperial power relations.[9]

This European-constructed "classical" Buddhism then, in turn, influenced "modernist"

Buddhism in Asia. As Gananath Obeyesekere and others have discussed, Theravada Buddhists in Sri Lanka have appropriated, with modifications, this "Protestant Buddhism" from the West, in reaction to British rule and Christian missionary pressure.[10]

Despite the newly dawning awareness of how western Orientalism has generated this "religion," the imperial production, and now widespread consumption, of Buddhism continues apace, only now focused on Tibetan Buddhism. This seems to be driven by much the same western individualistic spiritual quest. Yet, as the appeal of Enlightenment rationalism declines among Europeans and Americans, the more recently constructed Tibetan Buddhism appeals to westerners more for its exotic, imagistic, ritualistic aspects, in contrast to the rationalistic ethical aspects of "classical" Buddhism.

Europe's failure to penetrate and dominate Tibet politically only increased the imperial desire and fed western fantasies about the land beyond the impassable Himalayas.[11] Tibet had long been coveted as the repository of lost Sanskrit manuscripts and their accurate Tibetan translations, preserved from the ravages of time. Indeed, westerners viewed "Tibetan Buddhist culture itself as an entity existing outside of time, set in its own eternal classical age in a lofty Himalayan keep."[12] This culture, even monastic life, was full of embarrassing animism and power was monopolized by the monastic elite. But Buddhism, brought in from India, had somehow, according to Robert Thurman and Marilyn M. Rhie, "turned their society from a fierce grim world of war and intrigue into a peaceful, colorful, cheerful realm of pleasant and meaningful living."[13] Isolated and above the world, Tibet was possessed of a timeless wisdom, a land before the Fall. Surely it held the cure for an ailing western civilization.

In 1949, however, an imperial power finally succeeded in taking over Tibet—only this time the representative of modern materialistic empire was China. Tibetan Buddhism, the embodiment of the spiritual and the eternal, was desperately threatened. The German Tibetophile who took the name Lama Govinda articulated well how the crisis was viewed in the western press and even in academic circles: as "the struggle between spiritual freedom and material power, . . . between the faith in the higher destiny of man through inner development and the belief in material prosperity through an ever-increasing production of goods."[14]

Since the mass exodus of thousands of Buddhist monks into exile in India, beginning in 1959, two forces—western Buddhophiles and the Dalai Lama himself—have constructed yet another Buddhist religion. Besides the Buddhist texts in Tibetan translation already known, the exiled Tibetan monks brought with them additional manuscripts and living knowledge of and commentary on those texts. Given the danger that such precious wisdom could be forever lost, western Buddhologists, who were creating the new field of Tibetan Buddhism in American universities, mounted an urgent salvage expedition. The Tibetan monks and scholars, who had no sense of the importance of the texts to the rest of humankind and, indeed, had been allowing such texts to decay without proper care, could not be trusted with the treasures. To recapture the hidden wisdom of these texts, moreover, Buddhologists brought tape recorders to record and then textualize Tibetan Buddhist teachers' millennium-old knowledge from recitation and debate on these "texts" as oral tradition. More important for the new religion that was being constructed, western Buddhists and others keenly receptive to the Tibetan exiles, presented a welcoming image of how they would like the Tibetan Buddhists to be. Tibetans fled Tibet to find a safe haven in India, Europe, and North America only to find themselves and their country already there—in the minds of their only-too-eager hosts—an idyllic agrarian land of Lamas, endowed with secret ancient wisdom and ruled benevolently by a Buddha.[15]

The exiled Tibetans proceeded to accommodate themselves to this western artifice. Ironically, in an attempt to gain western support for the independence of their country they presented themselves in terms of the western construct of Tibetan Buddhism.[16] The lives of the exiled Tibetans imitated western projections onto Tibet. The Dalai Lama became the symbol as well as leader of this new Buddhist modernism, which represents a dramatic change from what was practiced in Tibet. In the homeland, which was never solidly unified, the Dalai Lama was the representative of only one faction and area. Only after the Tibetans had fled the land did they need to construct a *national-religious* identity in order to generate western support for Tibetan independence. The Dalai Lama had to suppress both his own clan deity along with certain practices in other Tibetan Buddhist factions so that all Tibetans could have a common, "orthodox" religion.

In his promotion of Buddhist compassion for the cause of Tibetan independence, the Dalai Lama described Tibet much as certain Europeans described it in the nineteenth century, as a preserve of wisdom.[17] What is enduring about Tibet, therefore, is Buddhism. But Buddhism, which was brought to Tibet by the great Mahayana masters from India, now means mainly the practice of compassion. The Dalai Lama is thus offering to the West what it has long projected and coveted, hoping to get his country back in the bargain. "It is my dream that the entire Tibetan Plateau should be a free refuge where humanity and nature can live in peace and harmonious balance. It would be a place where people from all over the world could come to seek the true meaning of peace within themselves, away from the tensions and pressures of much of the rest of the world."[18]

Tibetan Buddhism thus appears to float free from the Tibetan people's history and culture in a process of spiritual globalization.[19] Only in response to western yearning for a timeless Tibetan nirvana could Tibetan Buddhism achieve a coherent identity—as a timeless spiritual essence. As a product of empire, moreover, Tibetan Buddhism also adjusted to the shift from an empire of European colonialism to an empire of global capitalism that thrives on multiculturalism marketed as consumer commodities. The Dalai Lama has given the "Kalachakra," a type of tantric initiation, in mass-produced form over twenty times to over 250,000 people (e.g., in Madison Square Garden in New York City). And western-constructed Buddhism retains the textual form in which it was initially constructed, thriving among Americans with disposable income. When established publishers failed to recognize the growing market for Tibetan Buddhism during the 1970s, new publishers dedicated specifically to books on Buddhism and related spiritual materials sprang up in significant centers such as Berkeley and Boston. While advancing the textualization of Buddhism, these thriving ventures also furthered its commodification. "Classical" and now "Tibetan" Buddhism thus appears to be a prime example of religion produced by modern western imperialism, which is now being replaced by the empire of global capital. In the western-dominated construction of such religion, however, the history and culture of the people from whom westerners have abstracted and appropriated certain elements, have effectively become submerged and obscured.

Throughout this construction of Buddhism it is not difficult to discern a distinctively western understanding of religion. Westerners surely can benefit from the critical perspective of non-western observers such as Talal Asad. Several historical forces—such as the European colonial encounter with other peoples and their religions, the development of the sciences, the triumphant rise of capitalist relations of production, and the corresponding emergence of the modern secular state—conspired in the peculiar modern western separation of religion from political-economic life and institutions. The only legitimate space allowed to Christianity by post-Enlightenment society was individual *belief*. Religion in the West was reduced to individual faith and marginalized activities on sabbath days to keep it from interfering in the imperial industrial and capitalist reconstruction of the world on the one hand and, on the other hand, to retain it either as the remaining heart in a heartless world or a vague spirituality for nurturing sick souls. Caught in the comprehensive transformation of the modern landscape of power and knowledge, religion no longer served as a "constituting activity in the world." Religion became merely "a mode of consciousness which is other than consciousness of reality" generally. Alienated from the relations of production and no longer directly affecting the quality of political-economic-social life, religion became more of a privatized refuge and consolation.[20]

Given the reduction of religion to individual faith or spirituality, is it any wonder that many westerners feel that something is seriously lacking in their lives and in their society? The Buddhism constructed and consumed by westerners is deeply implicated in the imperial relations in which western elites, longing to be more complete and whole again, looked to subjugated peoples for the sources of their own salvation and healing—to Buddhist meditation and wisdom, to Native American sweat lodges and closeness to the earth, to African American spirit and vitality.

Professional training in and teaching of "religious studies" in American colleges and universities is also implicated in the western production of a "religion" that arose from modern imperial relations, such as "Buddhism." The construction of Buddhism and its inclusion among the "world religions" was heavily influenced by theological studies, out of which the study of religions generally grew. To qualify as a great "world religion," a candidate had to have a founder, an organized clergy, a canon of sacred texts, and a set of defining beliefs, although it might also have distinctive features of its own. With European imperial expansion during the eighteenth and nineteenth centuries, the list of "religions" gradually expanded, from

Christianity and Judaism to Islam, then Confucianism for its ethics, Hinduism for its mysticism, and finally Buddhism for its individual rationality.[21]

The prominent historian and theorist of religion Jonathan Smith suggested that religion is "the creation of the scholar's study . . . with no independent existence apart from the academy."[22] As the investigations of Buddhism by Donald Lopez and others demonstrate, the scholar's study has indeed played a highly significant role in the construction of a "religion" that constitutes a key component in American religious practice and the academic study of religion. Yet that is only part of the story. The construction of Buddhisms began not in academic study but in westerners' cultural-spiritual quests. Whole academic fields of textual-cultural-religious studies, such as Sanskrit, Buddhism, and Hinduism, then developed as secondary products. All such fields were deeply rooted in imperial relations from the outset, as Edward Said argued decades ago in *Orientalism*. Insofar as those fields and those "religions" have become institutionalized in universities and social practice, those who study and teach religion might heed Smith's call to "be relentlessly self-conscious," critical of imperial power relations as well as of their own social locations and roles.

2.

Devotion to Isis
in the Roman Empire

Both ancient and modern Eastern religion have fascinated western intellectuals. Two thousand years before modern Europeans "discovered" Buddhism, ancient Greeks and Romans adopted gods and religious rites that came originally from the exotic eastern lands of Egypt, Persia, and Judea. Modern western interpreters have usually approached ancient "oriental" religion with the same imperial attitude and stereotyped picture of the "decadent" Orient that they exhibit in dealing with more recent eastern religion. A standard book on the cultural background of the New Testament and Christian origins, *The Gnostic Religion,* provides an example.[1] In its "political apathy and cultural stagnation," the East prior to Alexander the Great had sunk into a "state of passivity, docility, and readiness for assimilation. . . ." But "Greece had invented the *logos* . . . the reasoned system—one of the greatest discoveries in the history of the human mind. . . ." Salvageable cultural elements could thus be "disengaged from their native soil, abstracted into the transmissible form of teachings." Babylonian religion, for example, because of the "catastrophes overtaking the East," was released from its "political function," forced "to stand henceforth on its spiritual content alone. . . . Political uprooting thus led to a liberation of spiritual substance."[2]

Modern western interpreters, however, tend to leave unmentioned and unexamined how it was that the "salvageable spiritual content" came to be "liberated." The "catastrophes overtaking" the East consisted of military conquests by the western imperial armies of Alexander the Great and his Hellenistic and Roman successors. Ancient Near Eastern empires had been contented to exercise political-economic domination over subject peoples. The Greeks and their western successors—the inventors of the *logos* and the source of that great civilizing force, European humanism—imposed a cultural imperialism as well, insisting that subjugated Near Eastern peoples adopt western culture. This combination of political and cultural imperialism is what forced the "liberation" of the East's spiritual substance from its previous "political function," thus making it "salvageable" by westerners endowed with the *logos*.

The statements cited above also suggest that modern western appropriators of conquered peoples' spiritual messages have ancient counterparts. Two millennia before German and

English intellectuals "discovered" Buddhism, ancient Greeks and Romans were eagerly borrowing subjected eastern peoples' religion and transforming it for their own purposes. One of those "liberated" bits of Eastern "spiritual content" was used in the Hellenistic and Roman construction of Isis mysteries. In fact, devotion to the transcendent goddess Isis, the Queen of Heaven, and initiation into her mystery rites became what a renowned interpreter deemed the high-water mark of piety in Greco-Roman antiquity.[3] That means that the Roman elites who became devotees of Isis, like modern westerners interested in Buddhism, were seeking personal spiritual transcendence in attachment to spiritual content appropriated from a subjugated Eastern people.

Temples to Isis and the mystery rites, and devotion practiced in Roman imperial society, were the product of centuries of imperial relations, something rarely discussed in standard treatments of the ancient Mediterranean world. For example, in connection with the extensive commercial contacts sponsored by the Athenian empire in the fifth century B.C.E., Egyptian merchants were honoring Isis in Piraeus, the seaport of the imperial center.[4] Elite Athenians were fascinated by Egyptian culture. As indicated in Herodotus's accounts, they acknowledged Egyptian influence on and similarities to their own practices and beliefs. Early on, Isis was identified with the heifer-goddess, Io, who, plagued by a gadfly, had wandered to Egypt.

The women's fertility festival in honor of Demeter, so similar to the rites of Isis, may well have been brought from Egypt.[5]

Egyptian religious culture spread more rapidly in the Hellenistic period under the Ptolemaic empire, founded by one of Alexander the Great's generals. In connection with their frequent founding of new cities (*poleis*), the Greeks had long since recognized the necessity of constructing a new "political" religion for the members of the "body-politic." Especially appropriate for the new metropolis of Alexandria, the Ptolemaic capital from which Egypt was to be administered, was some combination of indigenous Egyptian religion with the Greek culture of the Macedonian armies. As told by both the philosopher Plutarch and the historian Tacitus, Ptolemy I Soter ("Savior") elicited the aid of both Timotheus, a priest of the mysteries at Eleusis near Athens, and Manetho, an Egyptian priest from Sebennytos, where Isis was revered.[6] They collaborated in creating the cult of Serapis, a figure based partly on Isis' brother and consort Osiris. The temple of Serapis, erected under Ptolemy III, became one of the most famous temples in the ancient world. Insofar as Serapis was paired with Isis, the spread of his cult under the Ptolemies helped spread her cult. The merchants and the mercenaries of the Ptolemaic rulers were probably instrumental in this process. It is significant, therefore, that for a time the Ptolemies controlled many of the Greek islands and towns in the Greek mainland and Asia Minor where evidence for Serapis and Isis worship has turned up.[7]

As Rome gradually expanded its control of the East, Isis moved steadily into the West. The prominence she had gained in the Aegean shipping center of Delos helped her spread to Rome and the rest of Italy.[8] As "Our Lady of the Sea" (Pelagia), Isis guided the ships bearing grain and slaves from Egypt to the imperial metropolis. Those slaves, of course, some of whom later became freedpersons, may have been among the devotees of Isis, whose cult was most prominent in port cities such as Ostia. Although the Roman Senate, which had already given official status to the cult of the Syrian Great Mother Goddess, Cybele, attempted to suppress worship of Isis, devotion to her in private chapels and shrines gained adherents in high places. In 43 B.C.E. the triumvirate of Mark Antony, Lepidus, and Octavian had a temple built in honor of Isis and Serapis. During the great "civil war" between Roman warlords, the Eastern pretenders to power wrapped themselves in exotic Egyptian mantels, Antony posing as the incarnation of Osiris and Cleopatra taking the title of "New Isis."

Given the victory of Octavian as the champion of austere, traditional Roman gods and values, it may not be surprising that, early in Augustus's imperial reign (21 B.C.E.), Egyptian cults were officially banned, at least within about a mile radius of Rome itself. At the same time, however, even the mansions of imperial family members featured Egyptian decor and motifs. The knight Decius Mundus's scandalous seduction of the aristocratic Paulina in the sanctuary of Isis by pretending to be the Egyptian god Anubis suggests that the Queen of Heaven already had plenty of passionate devotees among the aristocracy in the Augustan age.[9] From the time of Caligula on, the worship of Isis enjoyed official imperial favor. Her temple compound on the Campus Martius in Rome was rebuilt and embellished by order of the emperors.

As indicated in such evidence as epigraphy and literary references, Isis enjoyed increasing adoration and attention in Roman aristocratic circles, including the imperial family, during the first and second centuries.[10] The night before the emperor Vespasian and his son Titus celebrated their glorious triumph over the rebellious Judeans—to take an example that connects with the subject of chapter 4 below—they spent the night in the temple of Isis on the Campus Martius.[11]

The devotion to Isis in the Roman Empire, apparent in Greek and Latin literature and modern archaeological evidence, is a new, perhaps even distinctive, religious expression, different from the function of Isis in traditional Egyptian civilization and from previous Greco-Roman religion.[12] Indeed, the transformation and reconstruction of Isis by the Greeks and Romans make it difficult to discern exactly what Isis's functions may previously have been in Egypt.

She was apparently one of the principal forces of nature-and-civilization that constituted and influenced life in Egypt under the Pharaohs. Behind Plutarch's western textualization of Isis and Osiris, siblings and consorts, can be seen the paired divine forces of fertility and productivity (related in some way to the Nile River and the land). Isis was primarily an active mother who, after seeking and finding her disappeared consort Osiris, generated and nurtured life. She was thus the generative force of Egyptian agrarian productivity and civilization generally. And since Isis was the generative and nurturing power it is no surprise that she was also apparently situated at the center of political power. She was both the mother of the god Horus, symbol of the sun and of monarchic order, and the throne on which Horus (embodied by the reigning Pharaoh) was seated.

Greeks and Romans identified Isis with goddesses and divine principles they were already familiar with, such as "daughter of Kronos and Lawgiver" (i.e., Demeter), Aphrodite, Artemis, Astarte, Cybele, Hecate, and (most curiously) "Latina,"[13] among the Persians. In numerous titles and phrases she is represented as the bringer of civilization in its many aspects. Most significant, however, was the transformation of Isis into a universal goddess and a force that transcended a world that was increasingly felt as confining, even enslaving. In an elaborate hymn praising of her powers from the city of Kyme she proclaims: "I am Isis, sovereign of every country." In her speech to the alienated and desperate Lucius, the main character in Apuleius's novella *The Golden Ass,* she asserts: "My single godhead is adored by the whole world . . . in different rites and with many diverse names."[14] While still a mother figure, she became elevated from her previously chthonic character in Egypt into the ethereal "Queen of Heaven." In an imperial universe in which even wealthy, leisure-class individuals such as Lucius felt vulnerable to deterministic divine forces, she became the force that transcended all others, the force that devised the courses of heavenly bodies, including the sun and moon. Besides compelling women to be loved by men, she became the Mother-Lover Savior who rescued individual souls from the otherwise unavoidable Fate (worshiped as a god in Rome)—the divine force that, judging from her ubiquitous statues and shrines, must have become increasingly prominent under the Roman imperial order.

Although Greek and Roman devotees of Isis identified her with all sorts of goddesses with which they were already familiar, Isis and her cult were also very different from traditional Greco-Roman religion. Greeks and Romans were clearly fascinated by the strange "oriental" exotica of the Egyptian goddess and the many associated Egyptian figures that decorated her sanctuaries. For example, Isis frequently wore between her breasts the distinctive folds of the Isiac knot, which reproduced the hieroglyphic sign for life (*ankh*). Sanctuaries were elaborately decorated with lavish reliefs, statues, and paintings of sacred animals and zoomorphic gods. Imagery of the cosmic order was also prominent, given her role of transcending this order, which seemed increasingly confining under the empire.[15]

The dramatic difference between the Isis cult and traditional Greco-Roman religion can be seen in the architecture and spatial arrangement of her sanctuaries relative to the rest of the urban world. Traditional temples in Greece and Rome were part and parcel of the public life of the city, open to and accessible to the main sites of public life such as the agora, or forum. People entered a temple directly from the public area to see the statue of the god(s) and goddess(es) and to view all kinds of sculptures, paintings, art, and offerings. Visiting a sanctuary of Isis, however, meant entering a secluded world, closed off from the surrounding public, urban life. As illustrated by both the Isis compound in Pompeii and the principal Isis compound in Rome, the sanctuary of the goddess stood in the midst of a courtyard that was enclosed by a perimeter wall, with no access from the street except through a narrow gate. The courtyard also enclosed quarters for those on "retreat" from the world or preparing for initiation, as well as for the priests. In her sanctuary, in the middle of a monastery-like compound, far from the gaze of non-devotees, Isis was thus inaccessible to the general public. The sanctuary itself offered an inner sanctum of an exotic, enclosed world in which one could gaze adoringly upon the statue of the goddess.[16]

This suggests that in order to assess the significance of various aspects of the Isis cult in the Roman Empire, a distinction should be made between the great Isis festivals and adoration of Isis and initiation into her mysteries. The "Vessel of Isis" festival, which marked the annual opening of the sailing season, at least in certain Mediterranean port cities within the Roman Empire, involved the general public in carnival-like processions. Yet as indicated in Apuleius's portrayal, only a fraction of the participants were actually devotees or initiates of Isis dressed in splendid linen robes, the women wearing veils and the men with shaved heads.[17]

Although the question of social location has occasionally been raised, little critical sociological analysis has been done on the literary, epigraphic, and other archaeological evidence for what sort of people became initiates or devotees of Isis. A survey of evidence for non-Egyptians in the Greek world for whom there is some record of connection with Isis prior to 30 B.C.E. identifies a substantial proportion from among the elite (scholars, statesmen, generals, courtiers, priests, ambassadors), some soldiers and lower-level officials, some artisans, but fewer from among the "lower classes."[18] Precise analysis of inscriptions by adherents of Isis and Serapis remains to be done.[19] The occurrence of slaves and freedpersons in the epigraphy does not warrant the claim that devotion to Isis covered the whole social spectrum, including the poor, in a representative way. Such evidence points rather to imperial power relations as a key factor in attachment to Isis. The slaves and freedpersons with some relation to Isis and her festivals may well have been from Egypt. Their adherence to Isis testifies to their persistence in cultivating their native culture.

Even in the absence of an adequate critical treatment of the social location of Isis devotees, key evidence points toward the higher levels of society. We have already noted imperial favor and the involvement of aristocrats and imperial family members. Archaeological evidence indicates that the Isis cult was prominent in port cities and along trade routes. It appears hardly at all in rural areas. Far from being taken as a sample representative of the rest of Roman imperial society, the evidence from Pompeii illuminates the distinctive demography of Isis devotion.[20] Pompeii was a "resort" town or elite "suburb" where wealthy Romans maintained "town-houses" as second or third residences. The "up-scale" profile of her devotees, therefore, is indicated not only by the appearance of Pompeian civic dignitaries and members of professional corporations among the adherents, but also by the fact that nearly a tenth of the population was in some way attached to Isis.

Apuleius's enthusiastic portrayal of Isis initiates participating in the festal spring procession as including "men and women of every rank and age," cannot be taken at face value.[21] He comments later that those chosen by Isis for initiation were generally the elderly.[22] And the considerable expense[23] that his character Lucius (an educated man of the nobility)[24] found necessary to lay out for his own initiation indicates that only members of the wealthy leisure class could afford the transcendent salvation proffered by the goddess. It seems clear, therefore, that intellectuals were prominent among devotees of Isis.[25] And while the majority of initiates were elite men, Isis was clearly attractive to high-status women as well. Whereas the traditional Greek and Roman religion reinforced the patriarchal-imperial order, devotion to Isis, particularly the asceticism she demanded, apparently legitimated a greater personal autonomy for women.[26]

We can distinguish three interrelated aspects of devotion to Isis among Greeks and Romans who became especially attached to the goddess: regular *adoration* of her statue or image; *initiation* into her mysteries; and an intense personal *devotion* or dedication to her as one's personal savior. The most elaborate source for these aspects, although not the only one, is Apuleius's portrayal of Lucius's transformation from his earlier life subject to Fate.

Isis sanctuaries were apparently open from just before dawn until early afternoon for the purpose of devotees' *adoration*. Most significant must have been the opening ceremonies at daybreak. Devotees awaited these anxiously:

"After the shining white curtains had been drawn, we prayed to/worshiped the adored image of the goddess, while the priest went around the altars set here and there, carrying out the divine service with exalted entreaties, . . . pouring libations from a sacred pitcher. Then when the rites had been duly performed, the faithful devotees greeted the light of dawn."[27] Pre-initiates and other devotees, as well as initiates and priests, were allowed to "enjoy the ineffable pleasure of adoring the image of the goddess" day after day "in gentle calm and exemplary silence."[28]

Initiation was not the result of any initiative on the part of the devotee, who had to be "called" by Isis herself, usually in a dream. In preparation for his or her (very costly) initiation, the devotee, before a company of already initiated *mystae,* was instructed by a priest from sacred books written in hieroglyphics, bathed according to Egyptian ritual, sprinkled with purifying water from the Nile, given secret instructions at the feet of the goddess, and ordered to abstain from meat and wine for ten days.[29] In the evening of the initiation, the devotee was led, in a virgin linen garment, into the holiest corner of the sanctuary where s/he underwent a 'death and rebirth' and a 'sacred marriage.' S/he approached "the frontiers of death" and the abode of the dead and then returned, having "approached close to the gods above and the gods below and worshiped them face to face."[30] The next morning, adorned in twelve robes and both a tunic and cloak lavishly adorned with otherworldly figures such as dragons, griffons, and winged animals, s/he was raised on a dias with flaming torch in hand and a crown of gleaming palm leaves—as a divine statue of the sun (i.e., as partner to Isis, who was the moon), in a sudden epiphany to the company of previous initiates.

Initiates' and others' continuing *devotion* to Isis was deeply emotional and entailed commitment and rigorous discipline. Apuleius represents Lucius in the most intense emotional release, weeping almost uncontrollably at the feet of Isis in the sanctuary. Long after his initiation, he kept the image of her divine countenance "stored in his inmost heart."[31] Lucius underwent two further initiations, including one into the mysteries of Osiris, after which he proudly shaved his head, but continued his duties as a successful lawyer in Rome. Many initiates maintained a strict asceticism, and some are portrayed in various forms of penitence. One woman reportedly walked on her knees over the coarse paving stones around the principal Isis compound in Rome. Another person traveled to Egypt to bring back water from the Nile.[32]

With our increased attention to the imperial situations in Greece and Rome, we may now surmise that intense adoration of and devotion to a divine figure, which was not typical of

Greek and Roman religion, may well have been developed in just such cults as that devoted to Isis, the "Queen of Heaven." The traditional, familiar civil religion had been renewed by Augustus and his successors precisely to reinforce the established imperial order. That imperial order, however, with power now centralized in the household of the emperor, became increasingly alienating to the Roman and other urban elites, who no longer played a creative and determinative role in the political process. It seemed to them that life in general now depended on the whims of the all-determining force of Fate. For some, only in an intense personal relationship with a protective divine lover-savior figure who came from outside the civil religion was it possible to find a personal, spiritual security and a sense that there could be any transcendence of Fate.

Greeks and Romans trapped in the empire appropriated, etherealized, and "commodified" the strange and exotic "Oriental" figure of Isis and her coterie of other Egyptian gods that enabled them to find inner spiritual security and transcendence. We may detect in Roman devotion to Isis certain elements reminiscent of contemporary "New Age" spirituality that appropriates indigenous peoples' religion to satisfy the personal spiritual hunger of the western leisure class. There are significant similarities between retreats, seminars, and workshops (available for a price) held in Aspen, Colorado, or Esalen, California, and devotion to Isis pursued in her sanctuary in Pompeii and the succession of costly initiations undergone by Lucius.

Greco-Roman adaptations and constructions of Isis religion have left many residues on western religion and culture. The Virgin Mary as transcendent, divine mother, of course, took over Isis's role and virtues as Queen of Heaven. Festivals held in May focused on the Blessed Virgin, whose statue was carried in joyful procession around the church or around the whole parish, bear remarkable resemblance to Lucius's portrayal of the spring ship-launching festival procession in which the statue of Isis was carried in a gala procession through the town. Similarly, statues and paintings of both Mary's nurture of her son, Jesus, and her grief over his dead body draped across her lap were adapted from the earlier statues of Isis nurturing her son, Horus, usually standing in her lap, and her grief over her dead consort, Osiris. The closest parallel in ancient literature to the modern Christian sense of Jesus as a personal heavenly Savior who loves and rescues the errant individual can be found not in the Christian Gospels, but in Apuleius's portrayal of Isis's love and rescue of Lucius.

Most interesting about the emergence of religion as individual faith and spirituality, however, is the lasting effect of the representation of the relationship Isis had with her individual devotees. Modern psychologists who were plumbing the depths of the individual psyche, particularly Jungian analysts, were fascinated by the "mythology" of Isis and Osiris and the initiation of Lucius into the Isis cult in Apuleius's *The Golden Ass*.[33] It appears that they simply rediscovered the striking parallels between the modern individual psyche and the ancient patterns that were instrumental in the cultural shaping of that psyche over time. The creative appropriation of a subject people's religion in the Roman aristocratic devotion to Isis was one of the primary causes of the emergence of individual spiritual transcendence in late antiquity. That same pattern of personal transformation and the crystallization of an individual self were taken over by the Christian cultural elite and lead fairly directly to the focus on individual faith in modern western culture.

Feminist criticism, finally, can illuminate yet another key aspect of the role that Roman elite devotion to Isis played in the individualization of western religion. As both the ancient sources, particularly Apuleius's portrayal of Lucius's relationship to Isis, and modern Jungian psychological theory indicate, the "mature" adult psyche is constructed as masculine by males. When Lucius, after his initiation into Isis, adores his lover-savior in his innermost heart, he is incorporating his anima, thus enabling him to become a secure and stable adult. Internalizing his transcendent, divine, feminine aspects enables him to leave behind the aimless, dissolute life of his youth and to become a successful lawyer in Rome. This masculine construction by ancient elite Roman males such as Plutarch and Apuleius conceives of Isis as playing an instrumental role in service of a masculine, andromorphic self. The divine Queen of Heaven, however, has been able to survive her cultural constructions by ancient and modern western males. In a way that parallels Roman women's search for transcendence over their alienating imperial culture, Isis is now being rediscovered and reconstructed by American women seeking to transcend their own alienating, imperial, andromorphic culture.

PART TWO

Religion in Resistance to Empire

Like Buddhism, Judaism and Christianity are the result of the interaction between western imperialism and peoples it subjugated. While the Buddhism taught in western universities and practiced by many westerners involves western constructions of Indian and Tibetan peoples' religion, however, Judaism and Christianity originated as indigenous peoples' reactions to imperial rule. People being so intensely motivated by their religion that they can carry out suicidal attacks on symbolic targets such as the World Trade Center and the Pentagon is hardly unprecedented. In many countries of North Africa, the Middle East, and Asia, Islam has undergone an intense revival in the last few decades. Because most westerners are embedded in a political economic system that prioritizes profits and consumption, marginalizes communal values and privatizes religion, they could not discern the implications of this revival among peoples for whom religion is not separable from political-economic life. Were we only to look for them, however, there are numerous historical examples of peoples' resistance to imperial rule rooted in and inspired by a renewal or transformation of their own traditional way of life. These range from, in modern times, cargo cults in Melanesia, the Ghost Dance among Native Americans of the western plains, and "subaltern" movements in British-ruled India, to what are standardly conceptualized as "early Judaism" and its off-shoot, "early (Palestinian) Christianity," in ancient times. One of the more dramatic recent cases is the Iranian revolution of the 1970s, which took the form of a revival of Shiite Islam. It is an example of what can happen when people refuse to allow their religion to be reduced to private belief and their lives to be determined by imperial power.

3.

The Revival of Islam
and the Iranian Revolution

The Iranian "revolution" in 1979 caught the Shah, the CIA, and the world press completely by surprise. Events in Iran confounded the standard doctrines about development and modernization as well as the prevailing theories of revolution.[1] One of the principal reasons for the widespread surprise was that western historians and social scientists simply did not know how to incorporate religion or cultural tradition into their theories, particularly the integral interrelationship of religion and politics. If we take the discourse of Iranians seriously, moreover, another principle reason is that western scholars failed to take into account the effects of western imperialism, including the possibility that a people might resist imperial domination.

Complex historical events such as the Iranian revolution resist brief treatment. Even a cursory analysis, however, can remind us how western

imperial actions evoked resistance that was
channeled into a revival of Shiite Islam. It can
also illuminate how anti-imperial power can
crystalize around traditional religious images
and rituals. Significantly, a key factor in these
events was the Iranians' refusal to accept the
western reduction of religion to individual faith,
which would have enabled an easier imposition
of a global capitalist political economy.

Indeed, if we recognize that the standard
western understanding of religion was a primary problem at issue in the revolution we
should reconsider labeling the revival of Islam
in Iran as "fundamentalism." The mass media,
controlled by a few multinational corporations,
deploy "out-of-scale trans-national images" in
their production of "the news" to define international relations in terms of simplistic "-isms."[2]
Frightened by the specter of "Islamic fundamentalism" we readily reject the "extremism" of
"fundamentalists" and identify with "modera-
tion" and "rationality," the ostensible "values"
of "western civilization." We thus also acquiesce
in the practices of the global corporations and
western political power. Essentialist concepts
such as "fundamentalism" block discernment
and understanding of the complex relations between western imperial power and the Iranian
people, which generated the revival of Islam in
Iran. The label of "fundamentalism" also keeps
secular westerners from recognizing the inseparability of religion and politics in the Islamic
tradition out of which Iranians generated revo-

lutionary religious-political power in opposition
to imperial power.

Imperial Impact on Iran

Traditionally in Islam, the will of God, as re-
vealed to the Prophet Muhammad in the Quran
(like the Ten Commandments in the Hebrew
Bible), pertained to all aspects of life, whether
at the level of the individual, the family, or a
whole people. The western powers' control of
Iran for their own economic and security interests, and their attempt to "modernize" and
"westernize" Iran threatened the traditional Islamic way of life in fundamental ways.

In the twentieth century, the Shahs of Iran,
at the insistence first of the British and then of
the United States, launched aggressive programs of modernization and development.[3] In
the 1920s Reza Shah Pahlavi attempted to impose a "modern" western-style economy and
polity on top of the old agrarian structures. The
effect was to further divide Iranian society into
two classes, the westernized wealthy elite and
the rural and urban poor, who were basically
ignored. In attempting to force his program on
the society, Reza Shah not only replaced the
time-honored Islamic law with secular law
codes, but imprisoned or even murdered opponents, including leading figures among the
Muslim clergy, the *ulama,* to whom the poor
looked for guidance.

After World War II, the western powers allowed Iran a brief experiment in representative government. But when the Majles (parliament), led by Muhammad Mosaddeq, attempted to nationalize the oil industry, which was owned mainly by British companies, in 1953 the CIA engineered a coup and restored autocracy, with the young Mohammad Reza Shah Pahlavi as its client ruler. The United States, which had seemed to Iranians to be the champion of its self-determination after the war, now stepped aggressively into the imperial role. In the heyday of U.S.-sponsored "development" the U.S. government made the Shah's dictatorship in Iran the model of modernization, a beacon of progress in the Middle East. Iran, of course, also happened to be an economic goldmine; 50 percent of its oil profits were taken by western companies. Development programs favored the wealthy, western-educated elite in the cities. The peasantry were ignored. The small traditional artisans and merchants were ruined. The divide widened between the wealthy and the poor.

In the 1960s, moreover, the Shah's rule became more autocratic and repressive, virtually eliminating political participation even by western-educated modernist and nationalist groups. The CIA and the Israeli Mossad had organized SAVAK (the secret police) in 1957, which proceeded to use torture and intimidation to control the people. Iranians generally felt betrayed and humiliated by the U.S. Many in the elite were increasingly estranged from their families as well as their cultural heritage, and many people felt like prisoners in their own country.

Events that led to the Iranian revolution represent an almost classic case of the spiral of violence:[4] *oppression* resulting from the Shah's imperially sponsored "development" evoked *resistance* and *protests,* which were then countered by sharp *repression* by the Shah's regime, in which many were "martyred." Amid deteriorating conditions, such sharp repression eventually touched off the "revolution" that toppled the Shah, a revolution that took the form of a revival of Shiite Islam and was largely nonviolent. By eliminating all forms of political participation and protest in escalating waves of repression, the Shah, in effect, forced protest into Islamic institutions and forms. Successive waves of repression blocked, debased, or sent underground liberal and moderate parties as well as leftist groups, and drove resistance in the direction of a revived Shiite Islam.[5] Mosques provided the only possible meeting places in which the coalition of resistance forces could meet, and they provided a ready platform for the communication of Islamic ideology. With civic space eliminated by the Shah in order to force development upon resistant Iranians, civil society moved into the mosques.[6] And when funeral processions were the only form in which people could express their outrage at the Pahlavi regime, political protests were fused with and indistinguishable from powerful ceremonies that resonated deeply with Shiite tradition.

Rather than recapitulating key events, but fully aware that the dynamics of oppression, protest, repression, and revolt were at play, we can focus on how Iranians of all walks of life responded to two sets of leaders: tradition-oriented clergy, particularly the Ayatollah Ruhollah Khomeini, and modernizing intellectuals, such as Ali Shariati. In different but parallel and overlapping ways, these two kinds of figures led the revival of Shiite Islam. This multifaceted Islamic revival sought the reunification of the spiritual with the social-political, and of contemporary life with cultural tradition, against the western imperialism that was forcing their separation.

Mullahs and Modernists: Rival Leadership, Parallel Programs

Much of the leadership of Shiite-inspired resistance to the Shah and his programs was supplied by teachers and students in the theological schools, the *madrasahs,* particularly in the city of Qum.[7] And increasingly the aging Ayatollah Ruhollah Khomeini became the principal, indeed towering, figure among them. In the mid-twentieth century most Iranian *ulama* were still conservative backers of monarchy or stood aloof from politics. Only a handful had been involved with the formation of a constitution early in the century and then, with the efforts of Mosaddeq and other western-educated but faithful Muslim leaders, the establishment of a modern, yet independent, Iran in the early 1950s. After the United States overthrew Mosaddeq and installed the Shah, the latter attacked both the *ulama* and the mosques. Although the clerics had good reason to resist for their own self-interest, the vast majority responded with quietism and accommodation. By the early 1960s, however, some of the more politically aware clergy began to speak out against the Shah's development program. They found a base among a sizeable constituency of "traditionalist" Muslims. While accepting the formal separation of religion and secular governing institutions such as the monarchy, which was traditional in Shiite Iran, they insisted on the application of Islamic law in all matters of society and state, such as marriage and education, and even in legislation. It was almost certainly the aggressive westernization entailed in those programs, under insistent imperial sponsorship, that drove leaders among the clergy to expand the purvue of Islam and to insist on their own political role as authorities on social political matters.[8]

The *madrasahs* in the traditional city of Qum, in particular, became centers of political discussion. And prominent among the teachers at Qum was Ruhollah Khomeini. In the early 1920s he had been a mystic also interested in politics, unusual in the quietist Shiite context. Prior to the 1960s he had been merely a reformer, not an activist. In his highly popular lectures at the Fayziyeh Madrasah during the early 1960s, however, he was shifting. Finally, in 1963, when the Shah's troops attacked the Fayziyeh seminary in the town of Qum, killing a number of students, Khomeini responded with powerful speeches criticizing the Shah for his injustice to the poor and for yielding to the designs of the United States. He even charged the regime with destroying Islam for the sake of oil (for the West) and selling out to its enemies. Khomeini was arrested. When thousands protested in cities all over Iran, many were killed by the Shah's security forces. Saved from execution by the intervention of several Ayatollahs, Khomeini was sent into exile. That dramatic and sustained confrontation with the Shah and his military became the enduring basis of Khomeini's leadership in Iran. He continued as the only cleric who consistently spoke out against the Shah and his program of westernization, regularly sending tapes of his speeches and his writings into the country from his exile in Iraq.

It is important to recognize, however, that the Iranian "revolution" was hardly produced by a few *ulama* such as Khomeini simply through their supposed "authority over the masses." Although the peasantry was not an active factor in Iran, in contrast to most other revolutions of the twentieth century, many

urban groups and factions became actively involved. Readily allied with the *ulama* because
of their shared orientation to Iranian-Shiite tradition were the *bazaaris,* the traditional "middle
class," whose interests the Shah's development
program had undermined.[9] Also significant in
the alliance were the recent migrants whom development programs had forced off the land
and into the cities. These were the "disinher-
ited" of Islamic revolutionary ideology. Renewed devotion to Islamic traditions supplied
the cohesion and identity that such uprooted
peoples sought—as indicated in the names of
some of their organizations, such as "Religious
Association of Shoemakers, of Workers of Public Baths, of the Guild of Fruit-Juicers, of Tai-
lors, of the Desperates of [Imam] Hosein."[10]
Most significant was the new middle class that
had emerged partly as a result of the Shah's
aggressive development programs. Had the
Shah allowed political participation, engineers
and other educated professional people might
have followed modernist reformist leaders in
striving for national independence and a grad-
ual move toward democratic enfranchisement.
Since the Shah's repressive measures increasingly blocked the path of political participation,
such people turned against the Shah and, more
decisively, toward a resurgent Shiite Islam.[11]

In attempting to understand the religious revival that was driving the Iranian revolution it
is thus essential to recognize that the western-
educated new middle class and elite came to

reconnect and resonate deeply with their own Shiite Islamic tradition. "Modernist" Muslims in Iran, as in other Middle Eastern countries, felt that Islam was equal to or even superior to other cultural traditions in its cultivation of science and social justice. It had unfortunately been distorted by the Arab caliphs as an instrument of conquest and then taken over by "clergy," who were not original to Islam, which had abolished all forms of mediation with God. Such "modernists" were prominently represented in both the traditional and the new middle class. The CIA overthrow of the elected nationalist government of Mosaddeq in 1953 prompted their entry into Iranian political affairs, in what were necessarily "underground" or religiously defined form, because of the Shah's repression.[12]

That the resurgent Shiite Islam driving the Iranian revolution cannot be attributed merely to clerical leaders such as Khomeini can be seen most dramatically, perhaps, in the crystallizing influence of Dr. Ali Shariati, a Sorbonne-educated philosopher–sociologist influenced by Emile Durkheim, Frantz Fanon (whose *Wretched of the Earth* he translated), Jean-Paul Sartre, and Louis Massignon (scholar of Islamic mysticism).[13] Shariati and other religious modernists were important particularly because they spoke to and for the strong anticlericalism in Iran, yet articulated a parallel revival of Iranian Shiite tradition.[14] Shariati, moreover, was able to articulate the resentments of the disadvantaged as well as to help members of the rising middle class "affirm their identity in a society politically dominated by what they saw as a Godless, Westernized, and corrupt elite."[15] From 1969 through 1972, he delivered lectures eagerly heard (or read in mimeographed form) by the western-educated young. Shariati's imprisonment by the Shah and early death shortly after he had gone into exile, presumably at the hands of SAVAK, contributed heavily to his influence as a martyr on the revival of Shiite Islam. Next to Khomeini, Shariati is the most influential figure in the broad revival of Islam that led to the Iranian revolution.

To appreciate how a revival of Shi'ite Islam became the driving force of the revolutionary events in Iran in the late 1970s, therefore, we should note how Shariati's widely heard lectures paralleled the preaching and writing of Khomeini. Although their efforts were not coordinated, these two leaders inspired a wide range of people to take religiously inspired anti-imperial political action in a heavily repressive situation that the Shah had systematically attempted to depoliticize.

Most fundamental for both Shariati and Khomeini was to attack the separation of religion from politics—an interesting indication of the extent to which even the terms of resistance were dictated by the western impact.[16] Since the nineteenth century, Iranian intellectuals had blamed Iranian backwardness (vis-à-vis the West) partly on Islam, particularly on clerical conservatism. They had sought a solution in separation of religion from politics, in imitation of the West. The Shah's attempts to force that separation in his rapid development programs, systematic propaganda, and sharp repression, however, evoked resistance. Both Shariati and Khomeini insisted that it was impossible to separate religion from politics. On the one hand, they opposed western-style secularization and materialism (communist as well as capitalist). On the other, they criticized the quietistic *ulama* who, in their reticence about political affairs, had distorted Islam by reducing it to private belief. The spiritual, according to Shariati and Khomeini, did not reside in a realm apart from social-political life. Humans were two-dimensional, with a spiritual as well as a corporeal existence. Correspondingly every polity must have a transcendent dimension. To split religion from politics was a betrayal of *tawhid* (unification), a fundamental principle of Islam. A return to *tawhid*, said Shariati, would heal the alienation of "West-intoxicated" educated Iranians. Through the rituals of their faith, Muslims could be transformed at a level deeper than the rational, on which the West and westernization relied so heavily.

Both the Sorbonne-trained philosopher and the emminent Ayatollah also placed great emphasis on Iranians becoming reconnected with their rich tradition and becoming part of the *umma,* the whole Islamic people. The latter was a purpose that transcended mere Iranian nationalism and encouraged a more universal sense of humanity. As a paradigmatic symbol for this identification with and immersion in the people, Shariati commended the hajj. The pilgrim would "feel like a small stream merging with a great river," would feel new life as part of the people, alive and eternal.[17] The western-derived ego of disoriented Iranians could thus be transcended in a wider identification with humanity.

Khomeini had always been a mystic, and for him, mysticism was inseparable from a concern for social-political affairs. The mystical quest would lead back into social-political activity. Indeed, a spiritual reformation was a necessary prerequisite to social reformation. In contrast to the more emotional Sufi mystics, Khomeini practiced and advocated a very sober mysticism. In preparation for political activity, one must first journey to God, in order to shed an obsessive egoism. True self-realization comes only in relation to a larger concern. Only through a sustained spiritual discipline could one prepare for engagement in political affairs, that is, to preach the word of God and implement the divine will in society.[18]

Both Shariati and Khomeini further stressed that Islam had to be expressed in political action, particularly against God's enemies. Illuminated by divine knowledge from the hajj, said Shariati, the pilgrim could rejoin political affairs. He insisted that even prayer should have a political thrust related to political action. The paradigms for political action by the faithful could be found at the fountainhead of the tradition. After all, the Prophet himself, Imam Ali (the first imam, or leader, for Shiite Iranians), and Imam Husain had all been political as well as religious leaders and had fought actively against injustice in their own situations. Prophetic of his own impending martyrdom, Shariati appealed particularly to Imam Husain, the last descendant of the prophet, who had been martyred at Karbala attempting to defend the filial succession of Islam against the usurping Umayyad caliph, Yazid.

As suggested in these paradigms, both the "modernist" philosopher and the "traditionalist" Ayatollah placed great emphasis on justice, which Shiite tradition had elevated to a fundamental theological principle. Since God himself is just and commands justice, the Muslim community (umma) cannot tolerate a tyrannical law or a tyrannical ruler. In what could be taken as a summation of his and Shariati's remarkably parallel messages to "modernist" and "traditionalist" Iranians, Khomeini insisted that "Islam is the religion of militant people who are committed to faith and justice. It is the religion of those who desire freedom and independence. It is the school of those who struggle against imperialism."[19]

The Recombination of Religion and Politics

The implications for Iran were clear, but not the timing. When Khomeini published *Islamic Government* in 1971, he was anticipating a two-hundred-year process of Islamic revival and reform. Events in Iran took the Ayatollah as well as western observers by surprise. And, powerful as the ideology of resurgent Shiite Islam may have been in the events leading up to the Iranian revolution, it is hardly a sufficient explanation or "cause" of those events. A far more sophisticated sense of the complex historical power relations, and a sense of how power works in ways not ordinarily taken into account, are required to understand how events unfolded in Tehran and other cities in the late 1970s. As noted at the outset, one reason that the Iranian revolution caught western academic experts by surprise was their reductionist view of history as consisting only of political and economic affairs. Obviously, a more comprehensive approach is necessary for understanding the web of factors in which "religion" and "culture" were inseparable from politics and economics in Iran under the Shah's forced modernization and westernization during the 1960s and 1970s. We can begin by focusing on four issues in particular: (1) how Ayatollah Ruhollah Khomeini played a focal, galvanizing role in the Iranian revolution as it increasingly took the form of a revival of Shiite Islam;

(2) how massive political protests against the Shah took the form of traditional funeral processions; (3) how the veil, seen by westerners as a symbol of women's oppression, could serve as a symbol of political-religious liberation for women participating in the revolution; (4) how the United States, as an invasive imperial power, assumed the traditional role of the "Great Satan."

Ayatollah Khomeini's Role

Khomeini's sharp criticism of the Shah in 1963 and his subsequent arrest and exile secured his central role in subsequent developments, and his continuing outspoken opposition and communication into Iran from exile secured his leadership. To understand how his speeches and writings galvanized people into deep emotional commitment and action, however, we must appreciate how his sermons resonated with deep currents in Shiite religious tradition and ritual practices. A vivid illustration is the rhetorically powerful speech he delivered following his initial criticism of the Shah, on 10 Muharram (June 3), 1963, the most emotionally intense day of the year for Shiites. Three aspects of Shiite tradition are particularly important to identify here. First, funeral processions are usually held forty days after a death. Second, the month of Muharram is a time of mourning and ceremonies, with passion plays and floats commemorating the martyrdom of Husain—the grandson and legitimate successor of the Prophet, the third Imam for Shiites—who had been martyred on the battlefield of Karbala by Yazid, the usurping Ummayad Caliph. Third, a traditional form of preaching, *rawzeh,* is used toward the end of sermons to elicit weeping by appealing to and identifying with Husain. Preachers used this device to evoke rededication to principles of Islam no matter what the difficulties.

In his speech Khomeini began with the *rawzeh* and represented the Shah as analogous to Yazid, whose murder of Husain was being mourned and memorialized that day. Other leaders, including modernists such as Shariati, also began turning processions and other ceremonies during Muharram against the Shah by interweaving references to current events with commemorations of the martyrdom of Husain at Karbala.[20]

In the same vein, it was the persona Khomeini presented far more than the programs he enunciated that led the way toward revolution.[21] Partly by his own and his family's history, he could cultivate a legend of distress that connected him with the martyrdom of Husain. His father had been killed by an agent of Reza Shah, according to legend. After a close scrape with execution himself, he had been banished in 1964. He then lost a daughter and a son to SAVAK. Pursuing justice in the face of persecution and martyrdom, he and his family legacy were thus easily assimilated into the tradition of Husain and the Shiite imams. Khomeini also fit handily into the creative tension between the national Iranian Shiism and the universalism of Islam, in which the umma is always far broader than a particular nation. So part of his appeal was that he represented a more universal idea that transcended narrow Iranian nationalism. From early on, Khomeini was also known as a mystic who could handle the always-dangerous power of knowledge. And he was a paradigm of asceticism, which in Islam was not a withdrawal from worldly affairs but a refusal to be seduced by materialism. He was uncorruptible. Finally, quite unusual among Iranian clerics, Khomeini spoke in the language of the common people, often using almost comic-book hyperbole. These and other aspects of a complex persona resonated with Iranians because they evoked emotional connections and juxtapositions with traditional images, values, and ceremonies.

Funeral Processions as Political Protests

Ritual mourning processions that were traditionally held forty days after a person's death repeatedly became occasions for demonstrations against the Shah. Since the security forces killed increasing numbers of people participating in these processions, they generated more and more processions that provided further occasions for demonstrations. Insofar as these processions were traditional Islamic rituals, the revolutionary demonstrations assumed a fundamentally Islamic form, with the people's frustrations and resentments being channeled into symbols and rituals deeply rooted in Iranian Shiite culture. Most poignantly, perhaps, the revolutionary fervor climaxed in 1978 during Muharram, invoking a popular vision of martyrdom—"a victory of the blood of the faithful over the sword of the Shah."[22]

As funeral processions and mourning ceremonies became the main form of political protest, the significance and political effects of these rituals were dramatically transformed from a self-flagellating appeal to Husain to intercede in individuals' distress, into an imitation of Husain as the model martyr in resistance to tyranny and godlessness.[23] "With each brutal crackdown perpetrated by government forces . . . the Husain-Yazid model seemed more applicable to the Shah's regime."[24] In the struggle against the Shah (a tool of American imperialism) a ritual that had been instrumental in the passive acquiescence of the populace to the dominant political order was transformed into a ritual of personally empowering active resistance to imperial power by collective action aimed at establishing a more just and humane social order.

The traditional Shiite legends and ritual performances transformed in response to repressive power became a unifying symbol system around which people of different classes and varying interests, including western-educated professionals, could rally. Political participation in a variety of demonstrations, public prayers, and paralyzing strikes was remarkably widespread in all sectors of Iranian urban society. "This was one of those rare moments when an entire nation felt it had taken charge of its own destiny."[25]

The Veil as a Symbol of Women's Liberation

Another unusual feature of the Iranian revolution was the remarkable number of women who, often urged by Khomeini and others, became involved in demonstrations and were among those arrested, tortured, and killed. Many women who were active in protests, including highly educated women who had long since ceased wearing the *chadur,* proudly donned the veil in symbolic protest against the invasion of western imperial culture, which was dehumanizing and exploitative of women, never anticipating how the conservative *ulama* would impose it later.[26] The veil had become a loaded symbol in the western-dominated Middle Eastern countries in the nineteenth century. Colonialist Victorian men, while tightly limiting the freedom of their own women, had fixed on the veil (which was clearly hiding something mysterious!) as a symbol of the general backwardness of Islam that blocked its path to (western) civilization, as well as of its oppression of women. In the defensive response of Middle Eastern Muslims, the veil came to symbolize "the dignity and validity of all native customs . . . and the need to tenaciously affirm them as a means of resistance to western domination."[27]

In Iran the Shahs had made the veil a central issue in their westernizing "reforms." Whereas Kamal Attaturk had only encouraged unveiling as part of his secular reforms in Turkey, Reza Shah ordered the police to use force in removing women's veils and carried out bloody suppressions of protests. As part of the White Revolution in 1963, Reza Shah "granted" women suffrage, but it was an empty gesture, given his suppression of all political participation and denial of human rights.[28] The Shahs' brutal westernizing rule became focused on the symbol of the forced unveiling of women to a considerable degree. In that repressive context, the revival of Islam was empowering for women as well as men. During the mid- and late 1970s new opportunities for women's religious education at various levels burgeoned dramatically. "Many women came to feel that Islam offered them opportunities for self-realization and self-respect which they had found lacking in the western way of life as they experienced it."[29] Studying Islam was regarded as liberating, not backward. In this context, then, (and without the later hindsight on what the clergy would do when they consolidated power in their own hands) it is not surprising that wearing the *chadur* became a prime symbol of protest against the Shah's forced westernization.[30]

The United States as "the Great Satan"

In the Quran the figure Iblis refused to bow down before Adam and became the "tempter." In Islam, Satan is thus more like the figure in Job, and not the same as the Christian Satan or Devil, who is the force or even embodiment of evil. In popular Islam the "Great Satan" plays the role of a tempter who draws men away from obedience to God and into sin and destruction.[31] In Iran, however, this significance is compounded by the cultural pattern of personal and societal struggle of the pure internal core against corrupt outside forces. Indeed, it is often further complicated by the myth of (the Shiite imam) Husain's martyrdom at the hands of the oppressive (Sunni) caliph Yazid. Conquest and domination of Iran by western imperial powers, from Alexander the Great and his Macedonian Greek armies to the Russians and the British in the nineteenth and twentieth centuries, were understood in terms of the struggle of the pure inside against the corrupting outside. The imperial power and its corrupting influence was easily identified as the Great Satan.

The United States stepped aggressively into precisely this role in the 1950s. Since the U.S.

had previously seemed to be a protector of the right to self-determination, Iranians felt terribly betrayed when the CIA overthrew the democratically elected constitutional government headed by Mosaddeq and installed the Shah. Then, with increasing visibility and high-handedness, both the "American government and business interests acted the role of the exploiter and corrupter."[32] They treated Iran as an economic gold mine. The U.S. embassy served mainly as a kind of brokerage firm, arranging lucrative deals and contracts for American corporations. Hundreds of American entrepreneurs and businesses made many millions in Iran in the 1970s, and not just by extracting the country's oil. Economic exploitation was aggravated by cultural imperialism. "For the bulk of the population the foreign orientation of everything around them—television, architecture, film, clothing, social attitudes, educational goals, and economic development aims—seemed to resemble a strange, alien growth on the society that was sapping it of all its former values and worth."[33]

Iranians revolted against the Shah, but they identified the United States as the ultimate source of the corruption—a role it played well, with its greed for the people's oil, its strong-arm tactics in economic development and exploitation, and "its imperious attitudes toward Iranians and Iranian institutions."[34] Despair alternated with rage as secularized and western-educated middle- and upper-class people, as well as traditional shop-keepers and artisans, identified the United States as the Great Satan.

Rethinking Religion and Power— Again

In order to understand the way Khomeini's persona resonated with the people and the way political protests against the Shah's repressive westernizing development program took the form of religious ceremonies, we must move well beyond reductionist western concepts of religion, politics, and power. Both Khomeini's persona and the large funeral processions-political demonstrations tapped tacitly into traditional images that had been central to Shiite Iranian culture for centuries and were regularly acted out in central religious rituals. Shariati himself, who combined western social theory with modernizing reform of Shiite Islam, suggested that the imams exemplified sociologist Max Weber's concept of charismatic leaders insofar as they articulated the residual desires of the people and led them in action. Khomeini, who was often compared to or identified as the new imam, was clearly a charismatic leader.

This leadership and its symbolic importance, however, cannot be adequately comprehended using only Weber's concept, even when understood as fully relational. As explained by Peter

Worsley, Weber's sociological concept of charisma illuminates how collective action by a people can result from a leader's articulation of ideas and a plan of action for discontent people in a problematic social situation.[35] Such concepts, however, do not sufficiently consider the historical dimension. In the case of Islamic revival in Iran, comprehension requires full awareness of the particulars of imperial power relations in the nineteenth and twentieth centuries. It is also necessary, as dramatized by the Iranian revolution, to appreciate the historical layering and depth of meaning in ideas, images, and rituals, and how they can condense around a figure, such as Khomeini, or rituals, such as funeral processions. This requires a subtle knowledge not simply of texts, but of cultural-religious symbols, images, and rituals, and the emotions they evoke. Something more than "scientific" analysis, however socially sensitive, is required to open up the historical depth of immanent meaning that underlies the tacit understandings members of a culture recognize and resonate with when those images and ideas are evoked. A counterpower can be generated by collective identification with and enactment of traditional images, symbols, and rituals against the imperial power of economic development and the attractions of the modern western lifestyle, which is backed by military repression. In such cases it is impossible to separate religion and power, religion and politics.

Like classical Buddhism, the revival of Islam in Iran is the product of modern imperial relations, although in an almost diametrically opposite way. Classical Buddhism was constructed by western elites in conformity with the modern western reduction of religion to personal belief, and partly to alleviate the loss created by that historically distinctive reduction. Shiite Islam was revived and transformed by Iranians in direct reaction not only against western separation of religion from political-economic life, but more comprehensively against the transformation of their way of life by western political-economic power.

The transformation of Shiite Islam in Iran appears in some ways to be an accelerated version of what happened in India under the British. During the last century of colonial rule political participation by Indians was eliminated. In response, Indians constructed their own "Hindu" traditions and the institutions of the new religion known as "Hinduism" in close interaction with British Orientalism and other western cultural forces, such as the Christian missionary enterprise.[36] In Iran, mainly in the three decades following the American overthrow of Mosaddeq, western-educated and middle-class Iranians, along with a few progressive *ulama*, generated a revival of Shiite Islam, primarily in direct reaction to the forcible imposition of western cultural and economic forms and forcible denial of political participation to Iranians. Against the U.S.-sponsored program to deny subject peoples their own cultural heritage as well as participation in shaping their own social and economic life, Iranian opposition took the form of a revival of the only sphere of life that remained available, Shiite cultural tradition and the ritual space and symbols of the mosques.

The Islamic state that emerged following the Iranian revolution, dominated by the clergy, must also be understood as the result of the historical imperial relations between the U.S.-sponsored regime of the Shah and the Iranian people. The periodically intensive measures of repression taken by the Shah to enforce his westernizing development program nearly eliminated effective political parties and forms of civil society other than activities in the mosques. Thus, when the Shah was no longer able to control the revolutionary surge, there were no organized political parties strong enough to provide an alternative to the clergy and the people loyal to them. Khomeini, moreover, used his immense prestige to advance the new constitution that vested ultimate authority in the Ayatollahs. The historical result, of course, was that in the face of hostile western imperial forces, the new Islamic state quickly instituted repressive measures not unlike those of the Shah they had toppled.

4.

Renewal Movements and Resistance to Empire in Ancient Judea

The revival of Shiite Islam in Iran provides an analogy that will help us understand the historical origins of what we now call "Judaism" and "Christianity." Christian theologians still project their construct of a unitary, monolithic, but ethnically parochial "religion" called "Judaism" that was succeeded by the more spiritual and universalistic "religion" called "Christianity."[1] The resulting essentialist discourse of "Judaism" among Christians persists both in the field of New Testament studies and in that of Jewish history just as the essentialist discourse of "Islam" persists among Orientalists. The separation of religion from politics, and the historical emergence of Judaism and its spin-off, Christianity, however, did not develop until late antiquity; these institutions are a long-range result of the Romans' use of political and military power to ensure that indigenous peoples' commitment to their traditional way of life not interfere with their submission to the imperial order.

Until the Roman destruction of Jerusalem and the Temple in 66–70 C.E., the situation in ancient Judea under Hellenistic and Roman imperial rule was somewhat analogous to Iran under modern western imperial domination. What modern Westerners usually think of as religion and politics (and economics) were simply inseparable in Judean society in the "second-temple" period (sixth century B.C.E. to first century C.E.). As in Iran in the late twentieth century, when western imperial powers and/or their client rulers threatened the traditional way of life in Judea, indigenous groups of scribal teachers as well as popular groups mounted intense protests and movements of resistance rooted in revival of their traditional way of life.

To understand such resistance it is necessary to understand the general structure of the imperial situation in ancient Judea. Following the Babylonian destruction of the Judean monarchy and Temple in the sixth century B.C.E., the Persian imperial regime set up a temple-state in Jerusalem (the "second temple") that continued as the imperial instrument of local rule for six centuries, eventually under successive Hellenistic and Roman Empires. Contrary to the standard view that Judea was stable, the successive imperial regimes regularly interfered in affairs in Jerusalem, where rival factions among the high-priestly aristocracy vied for imperial favor. A series of such interventions was perhaps the key factor in touching off the Maccabean Revolt led by the Hasmonean family in the 160s B.C.E. During the ensuing period of imperial weakness, the upstart Hasmonean regime in Judea aggressively extended its own rule over Idumea to the south and Samaria and Galilee to the north in an imitation of imperial politics.[2]

When the Romans finally took control of the eastern Mediterranean they installed the military strongman Herod over most of Palestine. Just as the Shah was the United States' favored dictator, so Herod the Great became the Emperor Augustus' favored client king. He engineered massive "development" in Palestine, building temples and whole cities (Sebaste and Caesarea) in honor of the emperor, and bestowed lavish gifts upon members of the imperial family and upon cities of the empire, all funded by tax revenues taken from his subjects. The high-priestly families, whom Herod elevated to power and privilege, became the ruling aristocracy in Jerusalem under the authority of the Roman governors during the first century C.E., building ever more elaborate mansions in the upper city of Jerusalem.[3] Both the Roman historian Josephus and rabbinic literature give vivid descriptions of just how predatory the priestly and Herodian aristocracy became in its collaboration with the repressive measures taken periodically by the Roman governors.[4]

The realities of imperial domination of the Judean (Israelite) people stood in stark contradiction to the older Israelite tradition to which it claimed to be heir. Although the official scripture of the Jerusalem temple-state (the precursor of the Torah) emphasized materials that provided grounding and legitimation for the Temple and (high-) priestly rule, it also contained early Israelite traditions of their independence under the direct rule of God. Central were the exodus story of God's liberation of the people from bondage to the pharaoh in Egypt and the Mosaic Covenant with their liberating God, which established a people committed to political-economic justice under the direct rule of God, that is, to the exclusion of oppressive human rulers. Among the almost completely non-literate Israelite village communities subject to the Jerusalem temple-state, the exodus and covenant were understood to be central features of their popular tradition.[5] This early Israelite tradition of the people's independent societal life under the direct rule of God became the basis for persistent resistance and rebellion against imperial rule.

The centrality of such early Israelite traditions in resistance to western imperial rule can be seen most dramatically in the Passover, one of three principal annual festivals in the Judean temple community, celebrating the people's liberation from oppressive foreign rule in Egypt. Although in second-temple times Passover was celebrated in Jerusalem under the oversight of the high-priestly regime, it nevertheless brought to the fore the conflict between the Israelite tradition of independence and the reality of imperial rule. This conflict vividly illustrates the utter inseparability of politics and religion for Judeans under Roman imperial rule.

> When the festival called Passover was at hand . . . a large multitude from all quarters assembled for it. [The Roman governor] Cumanus, fearing that their presence might afford occasion for an uprising, ordered a company of soldiers to take up arms and stand guard in the porticoes of the Temple so as to quell any uprising that might occur. This has in fact been the usual practice of previous procurators of Judea at the festivals.[6]

When the celebrants protested a Roman soldier's lewd gesture, Cumanus unleashed his troops in a violent retaliation typical of Roman rule.[7]

Judeans' insistence on their traditional (Israelite) way of life was far more serious than an occasional outburst of popular unrest. Just as the Muslim "clergy" provided leadership in modern Iran, so the "scribes and Pharisees" often took the lead in anti-imperial protests and other agitation in ancient Judea. To understand the meaning of this behavior, we must appreciate their position in the imperial situation of the ancient Judean temple-state. Since the high priesthood was the creature of empire, the incumbent Judean rulers were beholden to their imperial overlords and generally collaborative. Scribal circles, however, along with ordinary priests, whose very role was to guide the people in maintenance of the sacred traditions and traditional way of life, were always caught in the middle.[8] While they were dependent politically and economically on the priestly aristocracy, they were prepared to lead resistance if their high-priestly patrons collaborated too closely with imperial officials and/or policy. At points of extreme imperial imposition, certain scribal circles even made common cause with the peasantry. The standard modern oversimplification of complex ancient Judean historical realities reduces the most influential scribal groups of the late second-temple period to religious "sects" of "Judaism," presumably in distinction from the "church" of the Temple establishment. Historically, however, these scribal groups can be more appropriately understood as activists in the Judeans' struggle to maintain their traditional way of life against the incursions of western imperial rule. A review of the imperial relations to which the principal groups and movements—the Pharisees, Essenes, "Fourth Philosophy," and *Sicarii*—were responding will clarify their origins and purposes.

The recent revival of Islam and revolution in Iran are particularly helpful models for understanding the emergence of apocalyptic literature and the Maccabean Revolt, which constitute the watershed for subsequent Judean and Galilean movements of renewal and resistance in late second-temple times. Backed by the (Hellenistic) Seleucid imperial regime, the "western"-oriented high-priestly families carried out a Hellenizing reform in the 170s B.C.E., transforming the Jerusalem temple-state into a Hellenistic city-state. Resistance formed among scribal circles, cultivators and teachers of the people's sacred traditions, and the peasantry, under the leadership of ordinary priests, particularly of the Hasmonean family (see 1–2 Maccabees). A group of the teachers produced visions of God's retaking control of history (Daniel 7–12). God was about to judge the oppressive Seleucid empire and restore "the people of the saints of the Most High" to sovereignty (Dan 7:23-28). That is, justice was finally about to be established in Judean society with its life again directly under the rule of God. Over a period of several years, whether inspired by such visions or not, popular forces fought the imperial armies to a standoff, and regained control of Jerusalem and rededicated the Temple.

Despite the temporary "success" of Judean guerrilla warfare against the Seleucid armies, the basic imperial structure under which Judeans lived did not change. In fact, it was intensified under Roman rule. Yet memory of the temporary liberation helped inspire recurrent movements of resistance and renewal for the next three centuries. Resistance to the Roman Empire mounted by some Judean scribal circles and ordinary priests is analogous to opposition to the Shah and his western imperial backers by members of the Islamic *ulama*. Three of the four groups usually treated as "sects" of "Judaism" originated as movements of resistance to imperial rule or played a significant role in such resistance.

The Essenes—one branch of whom are now identified with the wilderness community at Qumran that left behind the Dead Sea Scrolls—apparently formed in protest against the Hasmonean reversion to imperial rule.[9] Their disillusionment and dissatisfaction with the "wicked" high-priestly rule was so severe that they felt compelled to abandon their previous priestly-scribal positions in society and launch a new exodus and renewed covenant community in the wilderness of Judea.[10] The movement sustained its renewal by withdrawing for several generations. Under Roman rule they became even more adamantly anti-imperial, conceiving of the Romans (the "Kittim") as the embodiment of satanic forces. They even rehearsed ritual warfare in anticipation of the eschatological cosmic battle between the demonic forces of darkness and the Kittim on one side and themselves and the divine forces of light on the other.[11] They also apparently anticipated that in the fulfillment of history, they themselves, having "prepared the way of the Lord in the wilderness" (stated in their Community Rule), would return to a restored temple-state as leaders of a renewed society.

The Pharisees are usually cast in modern religious scholarship either as the legalistic opponents of Jesus or as the precursors of the rabbis who defined "normative Judaism." Historically, however, they were significant mainly as mediators between imperial rule and ongoing Judean attempts to persevere in their traditional way of life. Whatever their own motives, Josephus's accounts suggest that they opposed the Hasmoneans's expansionist practices and their assimilation of Hellenistic, imperial, political culture in their political-religious role as interpreters and adapters of the laws of Moses.[12] Hundreds of Pharisees or Pharisee-like Judeans were crucified as martyrs. As political "realists," however, the Pharisees settled into a patient mediating role, attempting to facilitate the conduct of societal life according to the Torah while serving under Herod and the high-priestly families, who were maintained in their positions of power and privilege by the Romans.

According to the Torah, however, not only did all aspects of Judean life belong under the sole rule and will of God, but (like Allah) God insisted upon sole religious-political-economic sovereignty. This becomes clearly evident in the movement Josephus called the "Fourth Philosophy." (For his Greek readers, Josephus likens

these Judean groups to Greek philosophies, the
first three being Sadducees, Pharisees, and Essenes.)[13] This new movement, led by a teacher
named Judas and a Pharisee named Sadok, organized resistance to payment of the tribute
levied by Rome when it imposed direct imperial
rule on Judea in 6 C.E. Josephus explains that
they "agreed in all other respects with the views
of the Pharisees, except that they have a passion for freedom that is almost unconquerable,
since they are convinced that God alone is their
leader and master."[14] The pharisaic and scribal
leaders of the movement thus insisted that
Judeans could not possibly render tribute to
Caesar, since that was tantamount to serving
the Roman emperor and Judeans owed exclusive loyalty to God, their sole and direct Lord
and Ruler.[15]

We may presume similar motives among the
Judean teachers who formed the "Dagger Men"
(*Sicarii;* a *sica* is a curved dagger) in the 50s C.E.
They surreptitiously assassinated collaborative
high-priestly figures in the crowds at festival
time in Jerusalem. In the summer of 66 they attempted to place themselves at the head of the
nascent revolt. Rejected by the popular revolutionary forces in Jerusalem, however, they
retreated to the fortress atop Masada on the
Dead Sea and finally committed mass suicide
there rather than submit to continued Roman
rule.[16]

As with the Iranian Shiite *ulama,* for these
ancient Judean scribes and Pharisees it was

simply impossible to separate political-economic life from religious commitment to a deeply ingrained traditional way of life that refused to compromise with imperial demands. And as with modern Iranians, it was the imperial threat to their way of life that evoked such uncompromising commitment to their God and resistance to imperial incursions.

In contrast to modern Iran and more in accordance with standard theories of revolution, however, it was primarily the ancient Judean (and Galilean) peasantry who periodically mounted serious resistance and revolt against western imperialism. The recurrent popular protests, movements, and revolts constituted far more of a challenge to the Roman imperial order than the more limited and short-lived resistance by scribal-priestly groups. In these popular protests and movements as well, it is virtually impossible to separate politics and religion.

Many of the popular protests of which we have brief accounts clearly were either inseparable from a traditional religious celebration or touched off by a Roman imperial violation of sacred traditions. As mentioned already, protests often occurred at Passover, as part of the celebration of the people's liberation from previous oppressive foreign rule. Large numbers of Judeans carried out a remarkably disciplined, nonviolent demonstration against Pontius Pilate after he sent Roman troops into Jerusalem bearing the traditional Roman army standards featuring representations that violated the covenantal prohibition against images. And when the Emperor Gaius sent a military expedition to erect a statue of himself in the Temple (a representation—of a ruler with claims to divinity!), Galilean peasants mounted a massive strike, refusing to plant their crops, which the Romans and their client rulers depended on for their tax revenues.

Most of the widespread revolts and renewal movements took one of two social forms embedded in Israelite popular tradition.[17] First, in each of the revolts that erupted in every major district of the country at the end of Herod's highly repressive reign and the largest movement in the countryside of Judea in the middle of the great revolt in 66–70, the people acclaimed a king who would lead them. These were all popular messianic movements patterned after the earlier movements in which Saul, the young David, Jeroboam, and Jehu were acclaimed by their followers as messiah/king in order to lead them against the Philistines and other foreign rulers (2 Sam. 2:1-4; 5:1-3; 1 Kgs. 12:20; 2 Kgs. 9:11-13). In the middle of the first century C.E. a number of prophets such as Theudas and "the Egyptian" each led his followers out into the wilderness or up to the Mount of Olives in anticipation of a new divine action of deliverance. These popular prophetic movements were clearly patterned after the exodus led by Moses or entry into the promised land led by Joshua.

Both John the Baptist and Jesus of Nazareth belong historically in precisely this context. Judging from the fragments of his preaching and his practice of baptism, John was a popular prophet leading a renewal of the Mosaic covenant. Baptism was the ritual by which one left behind the previous breach of the covenant and committed to the renewed covenant people (Mark 1:2-6; Luke 3:7-9, 16-17). As portrayed in the Gospel of Mark and in the Q speeches, Jesus of Nazareth was leading a renewal of Israel, adapting the popular prophetic "script" of the new Moses-and-Elijah. This renewal featured a new exodus (sea crossings, feedings in the wilderness, healings, exorcism of alien forces), a renewed covenant (Mark 10:1-45; Luke 6:20-49), and a covenant meal (Mark 14:22-28), as well as condemnation of Roman and high-priestly rulers (Mark 5:1-20; 11:14–13:2; Luke 13:28-29, 34-35). Jesus, like John, was not founding a new religion, nor was he merely a religious reformer who merely carried out a "cleansing" of the Temple. Like the other popular prophets, he was leading a renewal of Israel over against its rulers, who were the local representatives of the broader Roman imperial order. The earliest Palestinian communities of the movement Jesus spearheaded, moreover, appear to have followed more or less the same agenda of renewal, as evident in the earliest gospel documents, the story of Jesus in Mark and the Jesus speeches in the Sayings Source Q.[18]

Even the ordinary priests, or at least a large faction of them, joined the adamant resistance to Roman imperial rule as discontent escalated toward revolt in the summer of 66. The priests, particularly the high priests, were always in a delicate position, serving in the political-economic-religious institution of the Temple, which was sponsored by the empire and which served as an instrument of imperial rule. The Romans had charged them with collection of the tribute, payment of which was a violation of the Torah and nonpayment of which was considered tantamount to rebellion by the Romans. After the time of Herod, the official High Priest was appointed (and often deposed) by the Roman governor. And under Augustus the practice had been established of sacrificing on behalf of (apparently not *to*) the people of Rome and Caesar himself.[19]

Nevertheless, in the summer of 66 the priests officiating in Temple services—led by a high-ranking member of the priestly aristocracy, Eleazar, son of the previous high priest, Ananias—declared that they would no longer accept sacrifices from a foreigner, thus rejecting also the sacrifices on behalf of Rome and Caesar.[20] The chief priests, nobles, and most notable Pharisees argued that such sacrifices had always been carried out, which seems likely given the role of the Temple in the imperial order, but the ordinary priests and their leaders, such as Eleazar, surely had Mosaic covenantal tradition on their side.

The prolonged conflict between the Judeans' insistence on pursuing their traditional way of life and Roman imperial domination came to a head in the great revolt of 66–70, which culminated in the destruction of Jerusalem and the Temple by the Romans in their efforts to suppress it. The revolt appears to have been basically a popular insurrection of Judean and Galilean peasants, along with many ordinary Jerusalemites and some regular priests, against their own high-priestly and Herodian rulers as well as the Romans. It seems questionable from Josephus's accounts whether some of the priestly elite helped lead the revolt or, as Josephus himself admits, pretended to go along in order to regain control of affairs (lest their Roman patrons abandon them).[21] In any case, the point of the Judeans' and Galileans' religious-political-economic commitment is still the same: that God must rule societal life as a whole, even though this was in direct conflict with imperial demands. Even after the Temple was destroyed, and with it the priestly and scribal factions based there, the Judean peasantry again mounted a sustained revolt against Roman rule in 132–35 asserting their independence as subjects only to God.

The Roman conquests of Judea and destruction of the Temple left a powerful impact on the surviving Judeans and Jews of the Diaspora. Blocked in their bid to regain independence under the direct rule of God, Jewish communities now maintained their traditional way of life by means of more passive resistance to the repressive and seductive pressures of Roman imperial rule. It was not until well after the Roman legions devastated Galilee and Judea and destroyed the Temple that the rabbinic circles that shaped later "Judaism" emerged. Some scribes and priests and apparently some Pharisees formed rabbinic circles in Galilee that gradually gained influence in the cities of Galilee and diaspora Jewish communities outside Palestine.[22] They developed distinctive dedication to the written and the oral Torah and the cultivation of Talmudic learning. Not until centuries later, however, did the rabbis manage to gain dominant influence over Jewish communities in general.

Meanwhile, Jewish communities in Palestine and the Diaspora concentrated on communal pursuit of their own way of life insofar as the Roman imperial order allowed, while avoiding actions that might aggravate their imperial rulers. This was far more than religion in the modern western sense. By maintaining certain social and cultural boundaries vis-à-vis the dominant imperial society, they were able to ensure solidarity among their communities. Jewish synagogues were far more than "voluntary associations" that met for worship. They were also the congregations of the local ethnic communities and the form of local self-governance whereby Jewish communities conducted their own socioeconomic life. The "prayer-houses" where they met were community centers as well

as sanctuaries for worship. What is usually
called "Judaism" has almost always been an
ethnic community, a people, as well as a religion, and almost always a people living under
the rule of an empire, usually Christian, such as
the later Roman Empire, the Holy Roman Empire, the German Reich, and the British empire.

After the Roman crucifixion of Jesus of
Nazareth as a rebel leader ("king of the
Judeans"), the Israelite renewal movement(s)
that he spearheaded among Galileans quickly
spread—first among other Israelite peoples such
as Judeans, Samaritans, and diaspora Jews.
Paul and other diaspora Jews then catalyzed
"assemblies" (*ekklesiai*) of the movement
among other peoples and cities of the Roman
Empire, including Rome itself. Paul even used
symbolism central to the Roman emperor cult,
such as "the gospel" of the "Lord" who brought
"salvation" to the world, as key symbols in his
gospel of Jesus Christ as, in effect, an alternative to the Roman emperor. In the divine "mystery" or plan for the true "salvation," God had
outwitted the imperial "rulers of this age." Para-
doxically, precisely in their crucifixion of the
"Lord of Glory," God had begun the final defeat
of the imperial powers. Enthroned in heaven,
Christ was about to destroy every imperial ruler
and power (1 Cor 2:6-8; 15:24-25). The book of
Revelation portrayed the Roman Empire as the
very embodiment of dehumanizing and de-
structive demonic forces. The communities of

Christ-believers, however, gradually assimilated to the Roman imperial order, and finally, under Constantine, "Christianity" was established as the imperially sponsored religion. The imperial imagery that Paul had applied to Christ as the anti-imperial Lord was easily transformed back into symbolism that supplied Christian approval and granted legitimacy to the imperial order.

Jesus had led a prophetic movement to renew Israel among Galilean and other villagers, revitalizing the traditional Mosaic covenantal principles of communal mutuality and justice, in resistance to oppressive Roman imperial rule. Within three centuries—and continuing into modern missionary enterprises largely overseen by western European empires—his movement had been utterly transformed into an imperial religion used to control such villagers, often by suppressing or subverting their traditional way of life. The central symbols of imperial Christianity, moreover, were easily transferable to new situations. The English colonies on the eastern seaboard of North America, who understood themselves as God's new Israel in an exodus from oppression in Europe, quickly adopted an identity as the new Rome once they gained their independence. The fusion of these two irreconcilable identities in America's conception of itself is now coming to climactic expression in the upsurge of American imperialism.

It is not clear what is gained by anachronistically projecting the essentialist "religions" of "Judaism" and "Christianity" onto their historical origins in subject peoples' resistance to western imperial domination in movements of renewal of the covenantal Israelite way of life. It is clear, however, what is lost. Blinded by their essentialist assumptions about religion, many modern scholars, as well as contemporary Jews and Christians, are unable to discern and appreciate the historical struggles against imperial domination in which Jewish and Christian histories and literatures originated. Also lost, of course, is the ability to recognize parallels between Jewish and Christian origins and the current struggles of imperially subject peoples to renew their own traditional way of life in the face of persistent western imperial encroachment.

PART THREE

Religion of Empire

Just as religion plays a prominent role in resistance to empire, so religion is used to legitimize empire. The importance of religion in cementing imperial power relations has been obscured both by the modern western separation of religion from political-economic life and by the assumption that politics, but not religion, is the arena of power. Such peculiar modern western assumptions must be set aside, therefore, to discern how religion can become a tool in imperial power relations. This will make it possible to recognize how, in significant historical cases, imperial religion is institutionally articulated in close connection with—indeed as an instrument of—the consolidation of imperial power. Imperial religion builds upon traditional religious forms previously associated with seasonal or agricultural cycles or civil society. Powerful figures at the apex of the empire and its subordinate institutions are able to transform such traditional forms into religious symbols, celebrations, and constructed environments that virtually constitute the much broader scope and scale of imperial power relations. With the help of recent studies by classical historians we can first recognize how this worked effectively in the early Roman Empire. Then, by analogy, it may be possible to discern similar developments in contemporary America, which has become the sole superpower, able to exploit the rest of the world for its own economic benefit.

5.

The Roman Emperor Cult

The modern assumption of the separation of religion and politics has tended to obscure the ways in which power relations operated in antiquity. It has become standard to think of power in narrow political terms, usually as if someone or some regime possessed power and subjected others. It is true that in the ancient Mediterranean world, the Roman patrician warlords commanded unprecedented military power by which they systematically subjected other city-states, peoples, and kingdoms. But once the conquests—and, in the case of intransigent peoples such as the Judeans and Galileans, reconquests—were completed, how was the vast empire held together? In an important recent treatment, a political scientist (who later became a consultant on U.S. "national security") explained that in a geopolitical "grand strategy" the Romans controlled its empire by skillful deployment of military forces.[1] Such an analysis, however, leaves unexplained the "civilized" core of the empire. It also fails adequately to consider how political-economic control is exerted through a pervasively influential culture and long-standardized cultural and social relations—what has come to be known as "hegemony."

The Romans did indeed maintain military forces on the frontiers to keep as yet "uncivilized" peoples such as the Judeans, Gauls, and Britons under control. In the civilized areas, however—such as the Greek cities of Corinth and Ephesus, where the apostle Paul carried out much of his mission—maintenance of the *pax Romana* required no military presence. Nor did the Roman imperial regime create and maintain a large bureaucracy as some other empires did. The *familia Caesaris,* the household of the emperor with its staff of "managerial" slaves, sufficed to handle the minimal administrative affairs. So in the absence of a credible military threat and a large bureaucracy, what held the empire together? Before answering this question one must understand why it had not been asked before.

Until recently western scholars could not even entertain the possibility that the emperor cult could have played an important role in the cohesion of the Roman imperial order. It simply "fell between the cracks" of the assumed division between politics and religion. It was neither fish nor fowl. Classical scholars, largely secular in their orientation, dismissed honors to the emperor as merely superficial religious expressions. Scholars of religion, working with a modern, western, Christian understanding of religion as individual faith, found it impossible to think that the ancients could have had personal faith in the distant figure of Caesar. Honors to the emperor must have been simply a matter of polite diplomacy in otherwise empty rituals. This reduction of religion to individual faith, of course, tends to exclude much that would be understood as integral aspects of religion in other societies, even to the extent that these aspects might be symbolized by and embodied in gods and goddesses: natural forces such as sky or earth (Uranus, Gaia in ancient Greece), political-economic forces such as war or irrigation (Mars, Ea/Nudimmud in ancient Babylonia), social formations such as cities (Athena), a people's rich cultural heritage (the Talmud, the *Iliad*, and the *Odyssey*), important communal practices or rituals (Passover, fasting during Ramadan), and even mountains and buildings (the Temple on Mount Zion, the Parthenon on the Acropolis).

Moreover, a questionable methodological voluntarism seems to accompany western methodological individualism, that is, an assumption that people have a choice about their religion. It seems highly unlikely, however, that people have much choice with regard to participation in already institutionalized festivals of their village, city, and society. People are born and socialized into those festivals. If those who effectively control them adapt and transform them, individual persons have little choice but to go along; they are simply swept along in the cultural stream.

In recent years a more relational understanding of power has developed. Power exists in complex networks and relationships that have various social and cultural-religious, as well as political and economic, aspects. Insofar as most westerners experience power at the capillary end of the circulatory system, they are still subject to power, and they are also capable of generating resistance.[2] This re-vision of power as "power relations" may not be as applicable to the ancient Roman Empire as to modern capitalist-industrial society with its pervasively effective "discipline" (learned in years of schooling and instilled in factories and offices). But the re-vision may enable us to discern previously unnoticed realities.

One such reality is the answer to the question above about how the Roman Empire was held together in the relative absence of military force and extensive bureaucracy. As some reflective classical scholars have recently explained, what held the Roman Empire together—indeed, what constituted power in the empire—was the emperor cult, operative mainly through image, ritual, and urban architecture. It also helped that the urban and provincial elites who sponsored the ritual celebrations also stood at the apex of a whole system of patronage headed by the emperor himself. But image and ritual did the necessary work—effectively.[3]

After decades of utter chaos during the Roman civil war, Octavian's victory at the battle of Actium over Antony, the demonic hero of

"Oriental" irrationality, seemed to re-establish cosmic order as well as political peace. In rapid succession following the battle of Actium, the magnates of the Greek cities began an elaborate transformation of the traditional Greek civil-religious institutions and practices and embedded in them significant new components. Statues of the emperor were placed beside those of the traditional gods in the sanctuaries of temples. Shrines to the emperor were installed around the *agora*—the public square, and principle locus of civic life—in each major city. New temples were built in the city centers. Long-standing organized games were renamed in honor of the emperor and new ones were founded and funded. Cities and provincial councils competed for the most elaborate and impressive honors offered to the emperor and his family members, judged by who could divinize him the most. In prominent public display the emperor was honored and celebrated as "the lord" and "savior," whose "gospel" of "salvation" and "peace and security" was publicly proclaimed. Although the emperor never visited these cities in person, the presence of the emperor came to pervade public space.

The very pattern of civic and economic life was restructured with its focus on Caesar as the divine source of life and savior of society and the images and symbols of his gospel inscribed on public monuments.

We should consider [the birthday of the most divine Caesar] equal to the beginning of all things. For when everything was falling into disorder he restored order once more and gave to the whole world a new aura. Caesar, the common good fortune of all, . . . the beginning of life and existence, . . . all the cities unanimously adopt the birthday of the divine Caesar as the new beginning of the year. . . . Whereas the Providence which has regulated our whole existence . . . has brought our life to the climax of perfection in giving to us [the emperor] Augustus, whom Providence filled with virtue [power] for the welfare of humankind and who, being sent to us and our descendants as our Savior, has put an end to war and has set all things in order; and whereas, having become god-manifest, Caesar has fulfilled all the hopes of earlier times . . . and whereas the birthday of the god [Augustus] has been for the whole world the beginning of the gospel concerning him, [therefore let a new era begin from his birth]. (OGIS 2, 58; inscription by the Roman governor and Provincial Assembly of Asia, 9 B.C.E.)

Elaborate festivals in honor of Caesar as lord and savior of the world were established in every important city of the empire. The Roman emperor cult was thus different from much

royal ritual in other kingdoms, which was usually centralized, often being performed mainly
for the benefit of the ruling circles themselves.
In the Greek cities of the Roman Empire, however, honors and festivals for the emperor (in
his absence) were performed for the benefit of
the urban populace in general. These cities were
representing the emperor to themselves, ritually
and monumentally constituting his presence in
their urban, that is, "political" life (*polis* in
Greek means "city"). Far from being foreign im-
ports imposed from on high, the images, rituals,
and festivals bestowing divine honors on the
emperor were developed out of traditional
practices in the Greek cities themselves, such as
sacrifices to local gods and celebration of re-
gional (e.g., Olympic) games.[4]

The imperial festivals became the high point
of the year, when the people could experience a
sense of community with their whole city. "As
part of the excitement, people streamed in from
the neighboring towns, markets were held, and
self-important embassies came from distant
parts. An imperial feast day was also a bright
spot in the lives of the poor. Rituals performed
for the emperor (who himself remained in
Rome) blended with high spirits and pride in
one's own city. For prominent citizens, it was
an opportunity to show off their own status and
how much they could afford to lavish on honors for the emperor and enjoyment of their fel-
low citizens.[5] By sponsoring all these rituals,
shrines, temples, and festivals the city and

provincial elite embodied and consolidated their own positions at the top of the Roman imperial order. They not only served as the "imperial priests" in their respective cities, but also occupied prominent positions atop pyramids of political-economic patronage, all headed by the emperor as the greatest patron of all—perhaps the most telling indication of how the religious festivals were inseparable from political-economic relations. The local elite expressed their generosity in ways beneficial to the people, many of whom ate meat only at such festivals. And in these elaborate rituals, feasting, and other public ceremonies in honor of the emperor, they were also recapitulating the local political-economic hierarchy.

These civil-religious ceremonies thus provided a privileged context within which the whole community was united in general gratitude to the powerful patrons. The wealth of the latter, of course, was almost certainly derived from their dominant roles in reproducing the very social relations that their sponsorship of the festivals served to veil. The wealthy magnates of each city thus simultaneously took responsibility for the community and for the gods, setting themselves up as the principle guarantors of community values. The urban communities thus also became dependent on the wealthy and powerful for the necessarily elaborate means of expressing appropriate piety toward the gods—including the emperor. These "imperial priests" became the mediators between the divine and the human as the very sponsors of the images and rituals that held the whole imperial order together.[6]

Most sobering for reductionist modern western theories of religion is the determinative significance of public space for the imperial cult. The entire urban environment of public life was pervaded by the presence of the emperor, as the appropriate architectural changes were made in city centers to accommodate new imperial temples in addition to the necessary new shrines and statues in the existing temples to the traditional gods. The presence of the emperor was thus permanently and prominently built into the spatial, visual, ambient environment.[7]

With the help of scholars of classical architecture and archaeology, along with some fresh theorizing about power relations, we are thus able to come to grips with how the Roman Empire was held together not so much by threat of military violence or bureaucratic administration as through the emperor cult generated and maintained by the subject cities. The pervasive and prominent rituals of the imperial cult constituted power relations. But it would be inadequate to conclude that, in the case of the Roman emperor cult, power worked through religion and not politics, perpetuating the separation between the two categories. Rather religion and politics—and economics, in the patronage relations that paralleled the emperor cult—were inseparable in the relations of power articulated and manifested by the images and rituals.

In order to understand this example of the religion of empire, one must acknowledge the most significant aspect of the Roman emperor cult: it was not imposed on the cities of the empire by the imperial regime. The initiative came from the Greek cities themselves and honors to the emperor were developed on the basis of those cities' own traditional civil-religious forms and festivals.[8] The Greek cities had previously honored the city of Rome and one or another of the great Roman warlords. But beginning with Octavian's victory at Actium, there was suddenly a new world-historical power central in the determination of their civic life. The images and rituals in the Greek cities acknowledged that the emperor was one among the many powers, in fact the most important power, that determined their lives and therefore must be honored and celebrated. Before long the emperor cult was established also in Rome itself as well as in the cities and towns of western areas of the empire.[9]

Religion and political-economic structure were therefore inseparable in the relations of power. The rapid emergence of emperor worship, built on the basis of the traditional Greek religion, and its spread throughout the empire suggest a theory of religion: that people worship or serve (or appease and honor—as gods) the powers/forces that impinge upon and determine their lives. In the Roman imperial order, the most important such power was the emperor, the symbolically real as well as politically-economically real figure at the apex of imperial power relations. What made the emperor a real presence in the central "civilized" areas of the empire was all the symbols, rituals, and ceremonies in which the imperial power relations were constituted.

6.

Christmas, the Festival of Consumer Capitalism

The recent recognition of the importance of the emperor cult in constituting power relations in the Roman Empire alerts us to the emergence of a corresponding imperial religion in our own "new world order." To recapitulate key aspects of the Roman imperial religion, the economic "movers and shakers" of the empire, transforming earlier civil-religious festivals, developed elaborate festivals celebrating the end-and-beginning of the year and the climax of the annual economic cycle. Public space itself was transformed, pervaded by the imperial presence in shrines, statues, and the facades of city centers. The imperial festivals were celebrations of abundance, with indulgence in feasting, drinking, and gift giving, with the most prominent economic and religious figures of the city presiding over the ceremonies as they displayed their largesse by sponsoring an excess of public entertainments that brought a sense of unity to cities and the imperial order. Given the reduction of religion to individual belief and of the marginalization of "religions" such as Christianity and Judaism in the modern world, we should be alert to other cultural and religious forms that, previously unrecognized, may have come to constitute power relations in the "new world order" under the *pax Americana*. And if we look, we find striking analogies to all of the features of the Roman imperial cult in the festival of unprecedented proportions developed in the United States and now being exported throughout the world: Christmas, or "the Holidays."

Christmas is often understood as a Christian festival. Indeed, some churches in colonial times did hold services commemorating the birth and incarnation of Jesus Christ. Yet the Congregational churches dominant in New England, bothered by the customary overindulgence and carousing, banned the celebration of Christmas until well into the nineteenth century. In fact most aspects of the celebration of Christmas in America as it developed into the principal festival of consumer capitalism had little to do with Christ or Christianity, as American social historians are beginning to explain.[1]

American Christmas built on, but transformed, the old European folk festivals that combined indulgence in abundance after the harvest with a celebration of light at the winter solstice to ward off anxiety about the renewal of life. One decisive step was taken in the early nineteenth century by the New York social elite, the knickerbockers, who had become increasingly uncomfortable with the custom of

wassailing, when the poor, who had in fact produced the abundance now in the storehouses of
the rich, demanded a few drafts of newly-
brewed ale and a taste of "figgy-pudding," in
the words of the well-known carol. So the
knickerbockers accordingly transformed the
age-old custom of wassailing into a domestic
festival of gift giving to their children in the privacy of their own houses. The conservative,
slave-holding New York patrician Clement Clark
Moore even composed a poem for the occasion,
"A Visit from St. Nicholas"—a completely be-
nign gift giver from whom the wealthy elite
"had nothing to dread." Seeing an opportunity
for profit, entrepreneurs began the process of
mass production of goods, such as Bibles, to be
given as Christmas gifts. Mass production
of goods gradually escalated into an orgy of
gift giving and consumption (*orgia* in Greek
meant "ritual"). The anti-commercial commercial icon of Santa Claus mystified the relations
of mass-production with the pretense that gifts
were hand-crafted and freely-bestowed by the
jovial, avuncular embodiment of free grace.[2]
The Christmas tree, borrowed from German
burghers, was transformed into the domestic
shrine for the celebration of abundance in gift
giving that expressed love and affection among
family and friends, thereby further mystifying
the burgeoning orgy of consumption.

From the outset of its development, therefore,
consumer-capitalist Christmas was grounded in
and also articulated the cycle of nature and

economic production as well as domestic affection focused on children. With the shift from family farms to urban areas filled with service industries and retailing, the American economy has become all the more dependent on and articulated by the climax of the annual festival of marketing and consumption in the Holidays. This orgy of gift giving, ostensibly an expression of mutual love and caring among family and friends, drives the consumption of vast quantities of unneeded goods, thus providing the all-important "spike" in the annual cycle of retailing. With people's desire whetted and channeled by intensive marketing during "the Holidays," the purchasing of gifts on credit cards at high rates of interest helps keep many millions of families, conceivably the majority, locked into their economically marginal positions.

Because Christmas has become so central to the American economy and American consumption is so central to global capitalism, this festival of "Holy Days" has become a central expression and embodiment of American *imperial* domination, an *imperial* religion. Americans consume the vast majority of world resources and Christmas provides not only a dramatic spike in the retailing that dominates the U.S. economy, but a powerful motivation to the whole enterprise of consumption of goods quite apart from human needs. Besides the dehumanization and impoverishment of other peoples, employed at minimal wages in the manufacture of unneeded consumer goods, the huge American drain on the world's resources has ominous implications for ecological sustainability.

American consumer-capitalist Christmas has become far more pervasive in public life than the ancient Roman emperor cult. Christmas decorations, lights, exhibits, and advertising pervade public space, particularly in downtown areas, malls, public buildings, and civic plazas. Christmas, however, pervades not only public space but the overall life environment. It appeals to all physical senses. Indeed, Christmas even invades our private space in a constraining way, particularly through advertising, and exploits every available medium of music and image as well as words. And we no longer have the freedom not to participate.[3]

American Christmas has also co-opted and incorporated American civil religion. As retailing for gift giving escalated from a few days to a few weeks to a whole "Holiday Season," Thanksgiving, the most important holy day in American civil religion—when families celebrate the foundational legend of the nation with a festive meal—became also the beginning of the prolonged Holiday festival. Mayors now preside at ceremonial lightings of city Christmas trees, celebrating at the local level what the President presides over at the lighting of the national Christmas tree in front of the White House, the residence of "the first family." City and town parades, like the nationally televised

Macy's parade, and Christmas displays that often combine Santa's village, reindeer, snowmen, and nativity scenes, further integrate the civil with the commercial dimension.[4]

That consumer-capitalist Christmas has become the dominant *religious* festival in American society is obscured by the ostensible separation of church and state and the assumed distinction between sacred and secular. This can be seen nowhere more clearly than in the artificial arguments and "opinions," of both the majority and the minority, in the 1984 Supreme Court case *Lynch v. Donnelly*. The Court ruled that it is not a violation of the (anti-)establishment clause of the First Amendment of the Constitution for the city of Pawtucket, Rhode Island, to include a nativity scene in a Christmas display of Santa's village in a public space.[5] Siding with the city, the majority opinion claimed that the purpose of the overall display had only the secular purpose of promoting good will and a gift-giving spirit among shoppers in the heart of the business district. In approving inclusion of the creche, one member of the majority specifically cited the need to solemnize public occasions through religious symbols and practices (e.g., prayers at public gatherings). While finding the nativity scene unnecessary for this purpose, the minority agreed with the general purpose of the display and the implied conflation of nation, patriotism, and consumer capitalism associated with Christmas, as a "secular" "holiday."

This relatively untroubled identification of a particular economic ideology and system with loyalty to the state is remarkable for what it simultaneously obscures and reveals: that ostensibly secular enterprise requires religious support and celebration. In both majority and minority opinions, secularity in this connection means a religiously neutral space that nevertheless employs religious symbols and practices in the service of the national identity and consumer capitalism. A previously distinctive Christian symbol thus becomes combined with "secular" symbols in solemnizing and enhancing a conflation of patriotism and global capitalism. To pretend that this Christmas display, with or without the creche, is "secular" rather than "religious" serves merely to veil, obscure, and mystify the emergence of what has become the dominant religious festival of American consumer capitalism.

The Christmas festival has become effective as an imperial religion precisely because it is understood as *secular,* as Kathleen Sands has argued convincingly.[6] In one of its principal contributions, the classic criticism of religion discerned that what are classified as "religious" rituals hide from view the political-economic forces that they legitimate or that find expression in them. We now need a criticism of the secular. As a set of "secular" rituals, Christmas hides from view its own *religious* functions, "so that the ambience and authority of religion can be surreptitiously transferred" to commerce and consumption.[7] Only as "secular," with its religious character and functions veiled, can Christmas become socially compulsory. Freedom to chose one's religion, including the freedom to participate or not in religious rituals and holy days, is one of America's most cherished rights. Yet we cannot refuse to participate in Christmas rituals of gift giving and receiving and other festivities without being socially ostracized. What makes the extended festival of the Holidays so overwhelmingly effective is precisely "the illusion that Christmas, unlike religion, is informal rather than formal, spontaneous rather than forced, based on our heart's desires rather than on social constraint or obedience. Not coincidentally, these are the very features that legitimate our political economy, . . . which "presents itself as an outgrowth of voluntary choices, natural or spontaneous desires, individual initiative, and impartial, nonarbitrary processes."[8] Only insofar as it is understood as secular rather than religious is Christmas able to hide the political-economic forces that it simultaneously legitimates and constitutes.

Structural-functional analysis has been appropriately out of favor in the last generation because of its inability to come to grips with social conflict and contradiction. Yet it may illuminate the functions of Christmas in the complex political-economic-religious system for which this festival was designed as a means of maintaining the cohesion of that system.

Among the interrelated functions that religion has served in many societies are the cultivation of personal and group identity, the establishment of community, and the articulation of an overall meaning of life. Given the reduction of functions and the social marginalization of churches, synagogues, and other religious organizations, it should not be surprising that Christmas has filled the vacuum in significant ways.

The festival of lights, gift giving, and the many special rituals (including television programs) in which American families participate during the Holidays from Thanksgiving to New Year's Day may be the key articulations of a sense of family for children. At all stages in personal life, festive family meals and gift exchanges during the Holidays secure family identity as well as family solidarity. Indeed, one's receipt of gifts at Christmas may be a primary articulation of individual identity insofar as commodities have become the generally accepted expression and measure even of personal value (including being valued by one's parents and loved ones) in modern capitalist society.

Participation, which is now quite involuntary, in the prolonged holiday festival also serves to integrate most Americans into the dominant American culture and identity, while still allowing them freedom to follow their ethnic and other religious customs (e.g., Hanukkah, Kwanzaa, ethnic foods). Throughout the Holidays, in performances, ceremonies, TV watching, or shopping in busy malls and stores, people have the sense of belonging and participating in a society-wide festival, being included in the whole, however frustrating the crowds are at times. Moreover, insofar as the Holidays have become the form in which the legendary founding of the society (Thanksgiving), the ending and renewal of the natural cycle (Solstice and New Year's Day), and the climax of the economic cycle are expressed and observed, this now complex festival articulates a general structure of personal and societal life.

Performances of deeply embedded "culture texts" in various media during the Holidays articulate "the meaning of Christmas." An excess of public entertainments in the mass media along with all the lights, displays, and advertising that pervade public and private space evoke the "Christmas Spirit" that inspires all the gift giving and consumption.[9] School and community choruses and orchestras give "Christmas concerts." School or community groups and professional theater companies perform Charles Dickens's "A Christmas Carol." Ballet companies perform "The Nutcracker" dozens of times (the revenue from which funds the rest of the ballet season). Hollywood makes Christmas movies (*The Grinch Who Stole Christmas*). Television networks screen Christmas specials as well as the already standard Christmas films such as *It's a Wonderful Life* and *Miracle on 34th Street*.[10] Many of these presentations, significantly, also serve to sell commodities and bring the annual economic cycle to completion. The American Christmas festival thus fulfills most of the major functions of religion in ways that collapse the supposed separation of religion, economics, and civil community.

Some have suggested recently that capitalism itself, or the capitalist market, is a religion.[11] That would be an oxymoron so long as religion is understood as *sui generis* or in the reductionist sense dominant in western society and academia.[12] It makes sense to discuss capitalism as religious (or as having a religious dimension) only insofar as religion is understood as integrally related to, perhaps inseparable from, political-economy—such as in the Holidays. As capitalism, in its ineluctable drive to grow, has begun to cannibalize previously separate institutions of the "public sector," it has increasingly developed features that we would identify as religious. Our task therefore is to analyze and understand the religious functions and effects of the consumer-capitalist system. How do the religious aspects of the global empire of consumer capitalism such as Christmas work in *constituting* contemporary relations of power?

In a highly influential definition, anthropologist Clifford Geertz described religion as "a system of symbols which acts to establish powerful, pervasive and long-lasting moods and motivations . . . by formulating conceptions of a general order of existence."[13] As anthropologist Talal Asad points out (with a nod to Marx), however, religion in this reductionist modern western understanding is "external to the relations of production, producing no knowledge, but expressing at once the anguish of the oppressed and a spurious consolation."[14] In the consumer-capitalist empire, where churches and synagogues and religious belief are so marginalized, the dominant institutions that produce the symbols, or rather *images*, that create "powerful and long-lasting moods and motivations" are the mass media, owned and used by huge transnational corporations. Far more pervasively and effectively than family and church or synagogue or mosque, closely interrelated advertising and programming in the media generate powerful images that supply individual and collective identity as "effects of power." In comparison with the religious forms of previous societies, however, advertising analyzed by itself would appear to be atomizing people rather than generating community and to be bombarding us with images that obviate the possibility of coherent meaning rather than "formulating conceptions of a general order of existence." Insofar as advertising and programming work in a broader cultural context as part of a whole system, therefore, our consideration and analysis must be more complex and comprehensive, for example, appreciating the effects of media advertising in the context of the elaborate religious festival of Christmas.

The capitalist market has increasingly taken over as the dominant source and measure of value and values. Increasingly sophisticated advertising has become the most effective means by which consumer capitalism pursues its religious functions. Far beyond anything Marx saw in the "fetishism of commodities," advertising has transformed commodities into objects significant not because of their intrinsic material, utilitarian, or esthetic qualities, but for their expressive power.[15] Working mainly through images and associations, advertising invests commodities with power to relieve anxieties, gratify fantasies, carry meanings, express feelings, and confer moral and spiritual value. By emphasizing the nonmaterial properties of commodities and associating them with the psychological and emotional needs and desires of consumers, modern marketing has mystified consumption in a far more fundamental way than Santa Claus ever did. Perhaps the most obvious way in which the religious function of advertising can be discerned, it skillfully plants a sense of inadequacy, insecurity, sin, guilt, or shame, for which it then presents the remedy (redemption, salvation, relief, absolution) in the acquisition of certain products. In consumer capitalism one gains salvation by the acquisition of products.

Advertising invests commodities with all these religious qualities and values primarily by production and association of images, which in previous societies have been the language and function of art, poetry, and particularly religion. Images and symbols, the vehicles for expression, recognition, and understanding of what makes us human—our primary communicative means for reaching beyond the boundaries of propositional logic and for contemplating the transcendent—are now produced and manipulated primarily by advertising in the omnipresent and invasive mass media.[16] For the purpose of "growing capital," advertising has relentlessly taken over as the primary (although not the exclusive) source of (non)identity and (non)meaning in consumer-capitalist society. Advertising has thus become the primary producer in our society of the (non)system of symbols and images that establish powerful and "long-lasting moods and motivations," that is, what Geertz meant by religion. Advertising manipulates desire in the capitalist system driven no longer by what Max Weber called "inner-worldly asceticism" but by inner-worldly satisfaction. But like the illusory happiness that Karl Marx saw in nineteenth-century "otherworldly" Christian piety, the ad-generated desire for commodities is really focused on illusory images that the possession of those material commodities cannot satisfy.

Only through consumer-capitalist Christmas, however, is it possible for advertising to effectively generate and articulate the "conceptions of a general order of existence." In order to do this, it must identify commodities as gifts that ostensibly express the purchasers' love and appreciation of friends and family, the virtual transubstantiation of commodities into spiritually salvific and morally redeeming objects to be acquired for purposes that transcend the utilitarian and mundane.

The market generates values as well as value in our society, but Christmas confers a kind of moral authority on these values. This is because at Christmas we purchase commodities for higher purposes—to express our love for others, our capacity for deep emotional feelings, our attachment to family—in the course of which we also participate in the wider economic and social community. By engaging us in the spirit of giving, Christmas validates and draws us into the spirit of consuming—which has come to replace what Weber had in mind as "the spirit of capitalism." The Christmas festival celebrates consumption, but it also nurtures the "moods and motivations" that keep desire for commodities strong throughout the year. As noted above, the Holidays constitute the climax of the annual natural as well as economic cycle, with its festival of lights, harvest, indulgence, and relaxation of standard discipline. Having transformed all those connections for its own purposes, Christmas is able to lend a magic and mystery to consumption that then carries over into the rest of the year.[17]

The principal factor that blocked New Testament scholars from recognizing that the emperor cult, in the absence of an occupying army and administrative bureaucracy, virtually constituted power relations in the Roman Empire was the Christian-determined modern under-standing of religion as personal belief. The modern religious fetish of religion as belief similarly prevents recognition of consumer capitalist holidays as the imperial religion that constitutes power relations today. Belief, how-ever, is as irrelevant to Christmas as it was to the Roman imperial cult. Several features of Christmas, of course, require a certain "suspen-sion of disbelief." Yet despite pervasive disbe-lief (e.g., in Santa Claus or in ads), the symbols and images of Christmas are highly effective in achieving the desired result: the massive pur-chasing of (unneeded) commodities for the orgy of gift giving and consumption. What does be-lief matter when the powerful presence of spirit and image is so pervasive that consumption is simply unavoidable? One participates like everyone else, with no real choice or faith-response involved. In the Roman imperial cele-brations of Caesar as Lord and Savior, of course, *fides/pistis* meant *loyalty* to, not "faith in," the emperor and empire. Similarly, in capitalist Christmas, regardless of whether par-ticipants believe in any of the symbols, cere-monies, or values involved, they express their loyalty to the capitalist system and its values in many facets of the festival.

Probably the most important way in which contemporary imperial religion, Christmas, dif-fers dramatically from Roman imperial religion is who, or what, it focuses on. The latter focused directly and explicitly on the emperor, whom Roman subjects honored and served in temples, shrines, games, and holidays, as the new super-human force (god) that determined their lives. In this regard the subjects of the ancient Roman imperial order were similar to the people of other ancient empires such as that of ancient Babylon, where political-economy and religion were inseparable. In ancient Babylonia the people were serving the primary forces that deter-mined their lives, such as Storm-Kingship and Irrigation-Wisdom, with their unpaid labor and the produce of their agricultural labor. In the Roman imperial cult, people were honoring the superhuman political power that determined their lives more than any and all other powers.[18]

In contemporary consumer capitalism, how-ever, the determinative power ultimately being served is veiled in mystification. It is effectively kept from entering consciousness. Most vividly in the Christmas festival itself, the cultivation of "the Christmas Spirit" in ceremonies, lights, music, and displays, along with advertising's endowment of commodities with spiritual pow-ers and effects, diverts attention from the power that is being served in the purchase of those commodities. It is imprecise at best to talk as if the market is god. The market is the economic system through which capital generates profits or growth, but the force Christmas identifies as determining life is capital. The religious fea-tures and festivals of consumer capitalism then serve to veil and obscure what, in both the market and its religious expressions, we are ultimately serving as the superhuman and supernatural force that determines our life. The god we are really serving in the celebration of Christmas is global capital.

... and a New Form of American Imperial Religion

The aftermath of the attacks on the World Trade Center and the Pentagon has seen the rapid resurgence of a distinctively American imperialism that may well be changing the operation of global capitalism. The symbolism of the attacks on September 11, 2001, clearly coincided with what had emerged in contemporary imperial power relations. The attackers targeted the World Trade Center as the prime symbol of (American-centered) global capitalism and the Pentagon as the central symbol of its military enforcement. Supported by the dramatic surge of American patriotism and anxiety about further attacks, the U.S. administration declared an unprecedented new policy of preemptive strikes and, in 2003, against intense international objections and without United Nations sanction, used its overwhelming military superiority to conquer Iraq. In contrast to previous hesitancy of Americans to think of themselves as an imperial people, the "neoconservative" strategists who have come to prominence in the U.S. administration eagerly argue that since American is indeed the sole world power, it should wield that imperial power aggressively.

There are ominous signs, however, that the effect of the U.S. administration's aggressive unilateral use of force may be disrupting or even undermining the international political-economic order carefully put together since World War II—the very order that made possible the empire of global capitalism. That is, whereas the United States previously served to enforce the new world order, it may now be overreaching in ways that bring about its disintegration. It is probably too early to predict how history will unfold as a result of the newly aggressive assertion of American imperial power.

Already evident, however, are signs of what might be an(other) American imperial religion—whose relation to consumer-capitalist Christmas is as yet unclear. As with the Roman emperor cult and consumer-capitalist Christmas, the burgeoning American imperial religion builds on earlier religious forms. The already imperialist American sense of "manifest destiny" was fed by a strong self-conception of America as a chosen people, God's New Israel, with a mission to redeem the world.[19] Early in the nineteenth century the identity of America as God's New Israel was fused with its identity as the new Rome, in the grand historic movement of empire from East to West. That sense of a God-given mission, of course, was easily transformed into secular form some time ago and rearticulated as "making the world safe for democracy." But it never relinquished its religious roots and aura. During the Cold War, the U.S. role was framed in a grand apocalyptic scheme of world history, as leader of the "Free World" against the Evil Empire of "Godless" Communism. After the collapse of the Soviet Union the mantle of the tyrannical "Evil Empire" was easily transferred to Saddam Hussein by 1991 and then, after September 11, 2001, to Osama bin Laden, and, in 2003, back to Saddam Hussein. In the aftermath of 9/11, the transmutation of the Evil Empire into the "Axis of Evil" was easily accomplished. And of course the identification of Arabic and Islamic countries and leaders as manifestations of the "Axis of Evil" has deep roots in the Christian Crusades against Islam. Finally, the signs of American imperial religion are evident in the U.S. administration's exploitation of support from the Christian Right, its initiatives that tend to collapse the separation of church and state, and its explicit use of language and symbolism with deep religious resonance in American culture, such as liberation, freedom, and mission. Prominent among these are the slogan "God Bless America" and the insistence that "God is on our side." In ways that parallel what happened in the Roman emperor cult, the newly resurgent American imperial religion has quickly come not simply to support the exercise of U.S. power in the world, but to constitute imperial power relations, at least in the United States body-politic itself.

Epilogue:
Religion as Effect of
or Response to
Imperial Power

It would appear that, as often as not, religion and other forms of cultural practice are embedded in political-economic power relations and—far from being reducible to them—reflect, express, resist, or even constitute those relations of power. In the historical and modern cases examined above, the way in which religious expressions form and develop depends on the particular configuration of imperial power relations. In both western-constructed Buddhism and the Roman aristocratic devotion to Isis, imperial elites adapted subject people's religion for their own spiritual transcendence of an unsatisfying life in the imperial metropolis. In both the recent Iranian revolution and ancient Judean movements and revolts, subjected peoples pursued renewal of their own traditional way of life in resistance to threatened disintegration by imperial power. In both the Roman emperor cult and American consumer-capitalist Christmas, the dominant aristocratic or corporate pyramids of political-economic power constructed an imperial religion that virtually constituted imperial power relations, making political and military power secondary in the imperial system in already "civilized" areas. It is simply impossible to approach or understand any of these cases as existing apart from the historical configuration of imperial power relations that they were attempting, respectively, to transcend, resist, or constitute and reinforce. In each of these cases of "religion and empire," religion appears to have been inseparable from, even the product of, particular imperial relations. These investigations of the relations between religion and imperialism have serious implications both for the study of religion and for religious people who are also active citizens.

In the study of religion we have a good deal of critical and conceptual work to do. It might be tempting, in our current deconstructionist drive, to conclude that religion is indeed simply the product of scholarly guilds. The modern Iranian and ancient Judean cases explored above suggest that religion cannot be dismissed as reducible to political and economic factors, much as the latter operate as influential factors in religiously motivated generation of social and political power. Nor can the problems exposed in the investigations above be addressed by working out a more satisfactory definition of religion. In fact, defining religion as *sui generis* may simply stand in the way of recognizing the various ways in which what may appear as "religious" expressions are inseparably related to other aspects of life. The various meanings and practices that we refer to as religious are always already in a context of political-economic and other relationships.

At least for the foreseeable future, as we strive to develop a more comprehensively critical understanding of religion, we must be thinking in terms of "religion and . . . ." The relation of the religious and the secular, for example, cries out for critical examination. Western secularism, with its pretensions to universalism, has been exposed as value-laden and contestable, as illustrated currently by the Christian Right in the United States and Islamic revival movements in the Middle East. Even certain historians and social scientists have recognized that secular nationalism carries many of the key functions previously understood as religious, precisely as it marginalizes and displaces religious institutions that previously carried those functions.[1] The relentless expansion of the American Holidays in the United States into a religious festival of historically unprecedented proportions illustrates how, in its secular pretensions, consumer capitalism has begun to collapse the previously institutionalized separate spheres of religion and civil society into a monolithic imperial system.

Most important, surely, given the establishment of the study of religion in western metropolitan universities, with its ingrained understanding of religion as individual and marginalized, is the religious studies field's inability to comprehend the relation of religion and power. If the study of religion were to recognize how religious practices are embedded in imperial power relations, then it might well serve a critical purpose in the new world order dominated by global capitalism. Recognition of the role of power in the modern western marginalization of religion, for example, enables students of religion to discern how construction and cultivation of religion primarily as individualistic spirituality, identity, and meaning tends to leave the operations of political-economic power uncontested and acquiesces in the commodification of religious expressions. Recognition of the disintegrating effects of imperial political-economic power on subject peoples' communal political identity and cooperative economic values enables students of religion to come to discussions of international relations with a more comprehensive perspective than, say, most political scientists or economists with their distorting Orientalist and secular reductionism.

Recognition, finally, that imperial power can generate and work effectively through its own religious practices can enable students of religion to develop a criticism of imperial power and its effects. In the field of biblical studies we are now becoming aware that in the cities of the apostle Paul's mission, the civic elite developed, out of traditional civil-religious materials, an elaborate set of temples, shrines, games, and annual festivals in which they rendered divine honors and faithful service to the imperial power that had come to determine their lives. Such historical cases can inform a contemporary criticism of the religious pretensions and effects of the power that determines people's lives today.

Neo-imperial global capitalism leaves the study of religion with new manifestations of religion and power to discern and delineate. It also places students of religion in an awkward task of defining our role. We could settle for serving mainly as curators of religious texts and rituals that have become artifacts left in the wake of imperial power. But we also may have something to say to power on behalf of cultural and religious pluralism based on the heritage of the very religious expressions and practices we study.

Churches, synagogues, mosques, and other religious communities, along with the clergy who serve them, while sharing many of the concerns just cited, may also have some of their own. Once aware of how religion can inspire resistance to imperial domination on the one hand and become the expression of imperial power on the other, American Jews and Christians may want to challenge the ambiguity of their own religious traditions. Most books of the Hebrew Bible, which is also the Christian Old Testament, in particular were evidently written by literate elites serving and articulating the interests of rulers and aristocratic institutions that were instruments of imperial rule. Many of the foundational Israelite cultural traditions included by those scribal circles, especially in the Torah and Prophets, however, give expression to the concerns and struggles of Israelite peasant groups against their rulers. As a result, the Bible "speaks out of both sides of its mouth," sometimes providing scriptural authorization for imperial domination, and at other times inspiring further struggles against empire.

American and other western Christians and Jews may well be especially concerned about the collapse of religion, civic life, and the economy evident in consumer-capitalist Christmas. This monolithic religious-political-economic festival is remarkably reminiscent of the ancient Roman imperial festivals. The recent fusion of religious-patriotic insistence that God bless America as it deploys its military power in the world is similarly reminiscent. This is a striking departure from the hard-won separation of religion and politics and economic life in western history, embodied in the separation of church and state in the U.S. Constitution. Ironically, the Jewish and Christian insistence on the transcendence of God and suspicion of practices that might attribute too much religious value to products of human labor or imagination may well have been a factor in the emergence of "secular" as well as "civil" religious expressions in America.

Ironically also, the insistence that no religion be established leaves the public sphere open for both civil religious and secular religious practices. The very secularism that supposedly protected cultural and religious pluralism now serves also as a veil for the religious functions of consumer capitalism. In its rise to prominence, consumer-capitalist Christmas co-opted and collapsed pagan, Christian, and Jewish religious observances (celebrations of winter solstice, Christ's birth, and Hanukkah) and the public space of civil society into the dominant capitalist order. And now global capitalism is co-opting and eliminating cultural pluralism even as it produces cultural diversity in commodity form. This power relentlessly eliminates not only natural species in its hunger for material resources, but also peoples and languages in its transcendent pretensions to universal control.

Most important for many will be the service of forces they do not consider divine, which rival the service of the force they do consider truly divine, the truly transcendent God. Many Muslims and Islamic communities today view consumer capitalism as a grave threat to Allah as well as to their obedience to Allah in pursuit of the way their religion calls them to live. Ancient Judeans and communities of Christ-believers refused to serve the Roman emperor insofar as it meant "rendering to Caesar" the "surplus" produce of their land and labor. The latter belonged properly to God, as "tithes," and God had designated such produce for the support of those suffering from poverty, hunger, and misfortune. Modern Christians and Jews have made various compromises with consumer capitalism. Yet the service of capital in the consumption of needless commodities that are merely images or fetishes of desire drives an increasingly unbalanced and unjust distribution of goods in the world that is now dominated by America and American imperial power. Just as the service of Caesar was rejected by early Jews and Christians as service of a pretentious false god, so contemporary service of capital through excessive consumption (like what used to be called "idolatry") might become unacceptable to their modern successors.

The new world (dis-)order is suffused with power and powers. Critical analysis and awareness of how these powers operate and the effects they have can help enable religious communities to respond self-critically as well as creatively.

Notes

Introduction

1. Edward W. Said, *Orientalism* (New York: Random House, 1978); idem, *Culture and Imperialism* (New York: Random House, 1993).

Chapter 1

1. Cited in Donald S. Lopez Jr., ed., *Curators of the Buddha: The Study of Buddhism under Colonialism* (Chicago: Univ. of Chicago Press, 1995), 5.

2. Lopez, *Curators*, 6.

3. Cited in Raymond Schwab, *The Oriental Renaissance: Europe's Rediscovery of India and the East, 1680–1880* (New York: Columbia Univ. Press, 1984), 71.

4. Lopez, *Curators*, 2, 6; Donald S. Lopez Jr., *Prisoners of Shangri-La: Tibetan Buddhism and the West* (Chicago: Univ. of Chicago Press, 1998), 6; Gauri Viswanathan, *Outside the Fold: Conversion, Modernity, and Belief* (Princeton: Princeton Univ. Press, 1998), 191, 206; Richard King, *Orientalism and Religion: Postcolonial Theory, India, and the Mystic East* (London: Routledge, 1999), 91–92.

5. Philip C. Almond, *The British Discovery of Buddhism* (Cambridge: Cambridge Univ. Press, 1988), 37; Lopez, *Curators*, 3–5; King, *Orientalism and Religion*, 64–72, 145–50.

6. Lopez, *Prisoners of Shangri-La*, 174.

7. King, *Orientalism and Religion*, 70–71.

8. Charles Hallisey, "Roads Taken and Not Taken in the Study of Theravada Buddhism," in Lopez, *Curators*, 44–46.

9. King, *Orientalism and Religion*, 149.

10. Gananath Obeyesekere, "Buddhism and Conscience: An Exploratory Essay," *Daedalus* 120 (1991): 219; Richard Gombrich and Gananath Obeyesekere, *Buddhism Transformed: Social Change in Sri Lanka* (Princeton: Princeton University Press, 1988), 307–11; Hallisey, "Roads Taken," 47, 60; Lopez, *Prisoners*, 185; King, *Orientalism and Religion*, 150–53.

11. This paragraph draws upon Peter Bishop, *Dreams of Power: Tibetan Buddhism and the Western Imagination* (London: Athlone, 1992), 34; Lopez, *Curators*, 252, 284; idem, *Prisoners of Shangri-La*, 5.

12. Lopez, *Curators*, 252.

13. Marilyn M. Rhie and Robert A. F. Thurman, *Wisdom and Compassion: The Sacred Art of Tibet* (New York: Harry Abrams, 1991), 22.

14. Lama Anagarika Govinda, *The Way of the White Clouds: A Buddhist Pilgrim in Tibet* (London: Hutchinson, 1966), xi.

15. Lopez, *Prisoners*, 184; Malcolm David Eckel, "The Ghost at the Table: On the Study of Buddhism and the Study of Religion," *Journal of the American Academy of Religion* 62 (1994): 1100–105.

16. The traditional ethnic identity of exiled Tibetans

thus becomes transmuted into a religious identity on western terms. As the Dalai Lama has observed, young Tibetans in the refugee community have a renewed interest in Buddhism because "Europeans and Americans are showing genuine interest in Tibetan Buddhism" (cited in Rodger Kamenetz, *The Jew in the Lotus: A Poet's Rediscovery of Jewish Identity in Buddhist India* (San Francisco: HarperSanFrancisco, 1994), 213. See also Lopez, *Prisoners of Shangri-La,* 196.

17. Lopez, *Prisoners,* 198, 200.

18. Dalai Lama, *My Tibet* (Berkeley: Univ. of California Press, 1990), 18.

19. Some of the following depends on Lopez, *Prisoners,* 175–78, 207.

20. This paragraph represents a condensation of Talal Asad, *Genealogies of Religion: Discipline and Reasons of Power in Christianity and Islam* (Baltimore: John Hopkins Univ. Press, 1993), 45–47.

21. Lopez, *Prisoners,* 161; S. N. Balagangadhara, *"The Heathen in His Blindness": Asia, the West and the Dynamic of Religion* (Leiden: Brill, 1994), chap. 8, 284–85, 307, 314; Peter Bishop, *Dreams of Power: Tibetan Buddhism and the Western Imagination* (London: Athlone, 1993), 91; Lionel M. Jensen, *Manufacturing Confucianism: Chinese Traditions and Universal Civilization* (Durham: Duke Univ. Press, 1997), 29–147; King, *Orientalism,* 40–41, 82–142; Peter van der Veer, *Imperial Encounters: Religion and Modernity in India and Britain* (Princeton: Princeton Univ. Press, 2001), 26–27.

22. Jonathan Z. Smith, *Imagining Religion: From Babylon to Jamestown* (Chicago: Univ. of Chicago Press), xi.

Chapter 2

All citations of ancient Greek and Latin texts are from Loeb Classical Library editions.

1. Hans Jonas, *The Gnostic Religion* (Boston: Beacon, 1958). The groundbreaking criticism of stereotypical modern western construction particularly of Middle Eastern peoples, cultures, and Islam—called "Orientalism"—is Edward W. Said, *Orientalism* (New York: Random House, 1978).

2. Jonas, *The Gnostic Religion*, 11, 13, 14, 15–16, 17, and 21–22. Jonas also realized that the liberating Greek *logos* imposed by the empires founded by Alexander and Augustus also had "another and profounder effect on the inner life of the East, . . . a repressive effect." Cultural elements that were unassimilable were "excluded and went underground, subjected to subterranean existence . . . an antagonistic undercurrent" (*Gnostic Religion,* 22). The previous two generations of Orientalist European scholars were less generous and less self-critical in their view of how "Eastern" religions invaded Rome, finding eager response among the emotionally susceptible "lower orders" and the demimondes who lacked the sophistication and rationality of the Roman elite, as noted by Sarolta A. Takacs in *Isis and Sarapis in the Roman World* (Leiden: Brill, 1995), 1–8.

3. Arthur Darby Nock, *Conversion: The Old and the New in Religion from Alexander the Great to Augustine of Hippo* (Oxford: Oxford University Press, 1933).

4. Robert Turcan, *The Cults of the Roman Empire* (Oxford: Blackwell, 1996), 81.

5. Herodotus, *History* 2.171.

6. Plutarch, *Isis and Osiris* 28; Tacitus, *History* 4.83.1.

7. Turcan, *Cults,* 81.

8. This paragraph is based on information in Turcan, *Cults,* 82–84, 86–87.

9. Josephus, *Antiquities* 18.72. Significantly, while the freedwoman who facilitated this seduction was crucified, he was merely exiled.

10. Turcan, *Cults,* 90–94. R. E. Witt, *Isis in the Graeco-Roman World* (Ithaca: Cornell Univ. Press, 1971), 238: "Isis enjoys the warmest imperial patronage [in early imperial times]." See the discussion and documentation of the cult(s) of Isis and Serapis as officially sanctioned under the Roman emperors from Caligula on in Takacs, *Isis and Sarapis in the Roman World,* chap 3.

11. Josephus, *War* 7.123.

12. The principal source for virtually all discussions of Isis devotion and initiation is book 11 of the satirical novella by Apuleius, *The Metamorphoses,* or *The Golden Ass.* Recent discussions of Isis dependent on this key source, however, have not taken account of the considerable critical literary analysis of Apuleius, *Metamorphoses,* and other ancient Greek and Latin "novels." The issues discussed in recent literary criticism are evaluated in E. J. Bowie and S. J. Harrison, "The Romance of the Novel," *Journal of Roman Studies* 83 (1993): 159–78. As Audrey Pitts has emphasized in an unpublished paper and private communication, the most serious failure of studies of Isis that depend so heavily on Apuleius is to realize that his story of Lucius, including apparently the portrayal of his initiation into Isis, is satire and cannot be taken at face value, particularly not as a direct autobiographical account. Read critically, however, satire can still be used as historical evidence, if we are fully aware of the likelihood of exaggeration, hyperbole, parody, and humor.

13. *Oxyrynchus Papyri* XI.1380.

14. Apuleius, *Metamorphoses* 11.5.

15. Documented in Turcan, *Cults,* 80, 108–9.

16. Documented in Turcan, *Cults,* 105–7.

17. Apuleius, *Metamorphoses* 11.8-17.

18. At several points in her survey of evidence, Takacs confirms my sense that serious devotees and initiates to Isis were not a representative cross-section of the Roman imperial population, but were concentrated among the elites (*Isis and Sarapis in the Roman World*).

19. L. Vidman did not index the *nomina* and *cognomina* from the inscriptions in *Sylloge Inscriptionum Religionis Isaicae et Sarapiacae* (Berlin: de Gruyter, 1969).

20. For the evidence from Pompeii, see V. Tam Tinh Tran, *Essai sur le culte d'Isis de Pompeii: Images et cultes* (Paris: Boccard, 1964), 60.

21. Apuleius, *Metamorphoses* 11.10.

22. Ibid., 11.21.

23. Ibid., 11.22.

24. Ibid., 11.15.

25. Witt, *Isis in the Graeco-Roman World.*

26. This is indicated in the appreciative comments as well as complaints by male poets about being deprived of sexual relations (e.g., Tibullus 1.3.23-32; and Propertius, *Tristia Solemnia* 1-6, 17-22). See further Sharon Kelly Heyob, *The Cult of Isis among Women in the Graeco-Roman World* (Leiden: Brill, 1975), and Ross Shepard Kraemer, *Her Share of the Blessings: Women's Religions among Pagans, Jews, and Christians in the Greco-Roman World* (New York: Oxford Univ. Press, 1992), 77. Takacs, *Isis and Sarapis in the Roman World,* 6–7, is critical of Heyob's thesis that Isis's feminine and

motherly features attracted more women than other deities of the Roman world.

27. Apuleius, *Metamorphoses* 11.20; cf. Martial, *Epigrams* 10.48.1.

28. Apuleius, *Metamorphoses* 11.22, 24.

29. Ibid., 11.22-23.

30. Ibid., 11.23.

31. Ibid., 11.24, 25.

32. Seneca, *Happy Life* 25.8; Juvenal, *Satires* 6.522-24.

33. For example, Erich Neumann, *The Origins and History of Consciousness,* trans. R. F. C. Hull (New York: Harper, 1962).

Chapter 3

1. As articulated, for example, by Samuel P. Huntington, W. W. Rostow, and Theda Scocpol. See, for example, Cheryl Benard and Zalmay Khalilzad, *"The Government of God": Iran's Islamic Republic* (New York: Columbia Univ. Press, 1984), and Mansoor Moaddel, *Class, Politics, and Ideology in the Iranian Revolution* (New York: Columbia Univ. Press, 1993), 2–22. Particularly considering how influential works such as Huntington's are on U. S. policies, it is all the more remarkable to consider how superficial and reductionist they are in minimizing the effects of previous history and of alienating foreign influence on political affairs in "third-world" countries, from his earlier books such as *Political Order in Changing Societies* (New Haven: Yale Univ. Press, 1968) to his recent Orientalist scheme in *The Clash of Civilizations and the Remaking of World Order* (New York: Simon & Schuster, 1996). One reason the Iranian revolution took U. S. "experts" by surprise is

that social scientists tended not to *read* the writings of opposition leaders, particularly not those they dismissed as merely "religious," as noted by H. E. Chehabi in *Iranian Politics and Religious Modernism: The Liberation Movement of Iran under the Shah and Khomeini* (Ithaca: Cornell Univ. Press, 1990), 34.

2. Edward W. Said, *Culture and Imperialism* (New York: Knopf, 1993), 309–10; Susan Harding, "Representing Fundamentalism: The Problem of the Repugnant Cultural Other," *Social Research* 58 (1991): 373–93; Mark Juergensmeyer, *The New Cold War? Religious Nationalism Confronts the Secular State* (Berkeley: Univ. of California Press, 1993), 4–6.

3. Analyses and discussions of the following developments are available in many studies, for example, Nikki R. Keddie, *Roots of Revolution: An Interpretive History of Modern Iran* (New Haven: Yale Univ. Press, 1981), 79–182; Said Amir Arjomand, *The Turban for the Crown: The Islamic Revolution in Iran* (Oxford: Oxford Univ. Press, 1988), 59–74; Misagh Parsa, *Social Origins of the Iranian Revolution* (New Brunswick: Rutgers Univ. Press, 1989), 31–90; Moaddel, *Class, Politics, and Ideology in the Iranian Revolution*, 29–97.

4. The original three-step sequence outlined by Dom Helder Camara is further developed into a four-stage "action and reaction" in Richard A. Horsley, *Jesus and the Spiral of Violence: Popular Jewish Resistance in Roman Palestine* (Minneapolis: Fortress Press, 1994), 20–28.

5. Chehabi, *Iranian Politics and Religious Modernism,* 38–39.

6. Ibid., 170–71, 184–85. The parallel with the development of participatory democratic "civil society" in dissenting churches in seventeenth to nineteenth cen-

tury Britain, from which it finally moved into the larger society, is striking. See further Peter van der Veer, *Imperial Encounters: Religion and Modernity in India and Britain* (Princeton: Princeton Univ. Press, 2001), and Richard King, *Orientalism and Religion: Postcolonial Theory, India, and the Mystic East* (London: Routledge, 1999).

7. Michael J. Fischer, *Iran: From Religious Dispute to Revolution* (Cambridge: Harvard Univ. Press. 1980).

8. Fuller discussion in Keddie, *Roots of Revolution*, 183–272; Arjomand, *The Turban for the Crown*, 91–102; Moaddel, *Class, Politics, and Ideology in the Iranian Revolution*, 154–63.

9. Chehabi, *Iranian Politics and Religious Modernism*, 91–97.

10. Ibid., 216–17.

11. Ibid.; Arjomand, *The Turban for the Crown*, 103–28; Moaddel, *Class, Politics, and Ideology in the Iranian Revolution*, 98–129.

12. Chehabi, *Iranian Politics and Religious Modernism*, 31, and chap. 2.

13. On Shariati, see, for example, Fischer, *Iran*, 154–67; Chehabi, *Iranian Politics and Religious Modernism*, 14–15, 47, 68–74, 187–89, 204–10; Shahrough Akhavi, "Shariati's Social Thought," in Nikki R. Keddie, ed., *Religion and Politics in Iran: Shiism from Quietism to Revolution* (New Haven: Yale Univ. Press, 1983), 125–44; and Abdulaziz A. Sachedina, "Ali Shariati: Ideologue of the Iranian Revolution," in *Voices of Resurgent Islam*, ed. John L. Esposito (Oxford: Oxford Univ. Press, 1983).

14. Chehabi, *Iranian Politics and Religious Modernism*, 14–15, 31, 47, 68–74.

15. Ibid., 99.

16. Compare with King, *Orientalism and Religion,* 82, 89.

17. Ali Shariati, *Hajj: Reflections on Its Rituals,* trans. Laleh Bakhtiar (Albuquerque: ABJAD, 1992).

18. The similarity of portrayals of Moses on Sinai/Horeb in Exodus 3, 20, and 24 and of Elijah in 1 Kings 19 is suggestive.

19. Sayeed Ruhollah Khomeini, *Islam and Revolution: Writings and Declarations of Imam Khomeini,* trans. Hamid Algar (Berkeley: Mizan, 1981), 28.

20. Chehabi, *Iranian Politics and Religious Modernism,* 72, 124.

21. The following is heavily dependent on Michael J. Fischer, "Becoming Mollah: Reflections on Iranian Clerics in a Revolutionary Age," *Iranian Studies* 13 (1980): 83–117; idem, "Imam Khomeini: Four Levels of Understanding," in *Voices of Resurgent Islam,* ed. John L. Esposito (Oxford: Oxford Univ. Press, 1983), 154–67.

22. Arjomand, *The Turban for the Crown,* 91–128; Moaddel, *Class, Politics, and Ideology in the Iranian Revolution,* 154–62.

23. Mary Heglund, "Two Images of Husain: Accommodation and Revolution in an Iranian Village," in *Religion and Politics in Iran: Shiism from Quietism to Revolution,* ed. Nikki R. Keddie (New Haven: Yale Univ. Press, 1981).

24. Ibid., 225–26.

25. Mohsen M. Milani, "Political Participation in Revolutionary Iran," in *Political Islam: Revolutionary Radicalism or Reform?,* ed. John L. Esposito (Boulder: Lynne Riener, 1997), 78.

26. Anne Betteridge, "To Veil or Not to Veil: A Matter of Protest or Policy," in *Women and Revolution in Iran,* ed. Guity Nashat (Boulder: Westview, 1983),

109–28; Haleh Esfandiari, *Reconstructed Lives: Women and Iran's Islamic Revolution* (Baltimore: Johns Hopkins Univ. Press, 1997), 5–9, 39–51. On "the discourse of the veil," see further Leila Ahmed, *Women and Gender in Islam: Historical Roots of a Modern Debate* (New Haven: Yale Univ. Press, 1992), 144–68, 222–28, 235–48.

27. Ahmed, *Women and Gender in Islam,* 151–52, 164. On the issue of the veil see further Ansuar Majid, "The Politics of Feminism in Islam," *Signs* 23 (1998): 321–62; Fadwa El Guindi, *Veil: Modesty, Privacy, Resistance* (Oxford: Berg, 1999); Lila Abu-Lughod, ed., *Remaking Women: Feminism and Modernity in the Middle East* (Princeton: Princeton Univ. Press, 1998), introduction.

28. Haideh Moghissi, *Populism and Feminism in Iran: Women's Struggle in a Male-Defined Revolutionary Movement* (New York: St. Martin's, 1994), 37–53; Guity Nashat, "Women in Pre-revolutionary Iran: A Historical Overview," in *Women and Revolution in Iran,* 5–35.

29. Betteridge, "To Veil or Not to Veil," 109–10. The definition of demonstrations as religious activity enabled many women to participate in them. See Mary Hegland, "Aliabad Women: Revolution as Religious Activity," in *Women and Revolution in Iran,* 171–94.

30. Betteridge, "To Veil or Not to Veil," 121.

31. William Beeman, "Images of the Great Satan: Representations of the United States in the Iranian Revolution," in *Religion and Politics in Iran,* 193–97.

32. Beeman, "Images of the Great Satan," 202–3.

33. Ibid., 209–10.

34. Ibid., 216.

35. Peter Worsley, "Preface to the Revised Edition," in *The Trumpet Shall Sound: A Study of "Cargo" Cults*

in Melanesia, 2nd ed. (London: MacGibbon & Kee, 1968). Compare Karl Mannheim's "utopian mentality," which opens up the interrelationship of a leader who articulates utopian ideas on which discontent people take action to change an intolerable situation, in *Ideology and Utopia: An Introduction to the Sociology of Knowledge* (New York: Harcourt, Brace, 1936).

36. van der Veer, *Imperial Encounters,* 30–54.

Chapter 4

All citations of ancient Greek and Latin texts are from Loeb Classical Library editions.

1. The standard synthetic and essentialist Christian scholarly concept of "Judaism" constructed in the late nineteenth century can be seen basically unchanged, for example, in Martin Hengel, *Judaism and Hellenism: Studies in Their Encounter in Palestine during the Early Hellenistic Period,* trans. John Bowden (Philadelphia: Fortress Press, 1974), esp. 303–9. A more nuanced but still monolithic picture of "Judaism" is constructed in E. P Sanders, *Judaism: Practice and Belief 63 B.C.E.–66 C.E.* (Philadelphia: Trinity Press International, 1992).

2. For a detailed reconstruction of this history, see, for example, Jon L. Berquist, *Judaism in Persia's Shadow: A Social and Historical Approach* (Minneapolis: Fortress Press, 1995); Charles E. Carter, *The Emergence of Yehud in the Persian Period: A Social and Demographic Study* (Sheffield: Sheffield Academic, 1999); and Richard A. Horsley, *Galilee: History, Politics, People* (Valley Forge: Trinity Press International, 1995).

3. Richard A Horsley, "High Priests and the Politics of Roman Palestine," *Journal for the Study of Judaism* 17 (1986): 23–55; Horsley, *Galilee,* 132–34; Martin

Goodman, *The Ruling Class of Judea: The Origins of the Jewish Revolt against Rome, A.D. 66–70* (Cambridge: Cambridge Univ. Press, 1987).

4. Josephus, *Jewish Antiquities* 20.181, 206–7, 214; *Yerushalmi Pesahim* 57a. See further Richard A. Horsley, *Jesus and the Spiral of Violence: Popular Jewish Resistance in Roman Palestine* (Mineapolis: Fortress Press, 1994), 29–33, 43–49.

5. An exploration of Israelite popular tradition in Galilee and Judea appears in Horsley, *Galilee,* 148–56, and Richard A. Horsley and Jonathan A Draper, *Whoever Hears You Hears Me: Prophets, Performance, and Tradition in Q* (Harrisburg: Trinity Press International, 1999), chaps. 5, 9, 10, 13.

6. Josephus, *Antiquities* 20.106–7; cf. Josephus, *War* 2.223–24.

7. Josephus, *War* 2.226. See further Horsley, *Jesus and the Spiral of Violence,* 34–35.

8. See further Richard A. Horsley and Patrick Tiller, "Ben Sira and the Sociology of the Second Temple," in *Second Temple Studies III: Studies in Politics, Class and Material Culture,* ed. Philip R. Davies and John M. Halligan, (Journal for the Study of the Old Testament Supplement Series 340; Sheffield: Sheffield Academic, 2002), 74–107.

9. According to the still dominant scholarly reconstruction (see, e.g., Geza Vermes, *The Complete Dead Sea Scrolls in English* (New York: Allen Lane, 1997), 49–66; James C. VanderKam, *The Dead Sea Scrolls Today* (Grand Rapids: Eerdmans, 1994), 99–108; Lawrence H. Schiffman, *Reclaiming the Dead Sea Scrolls: The History of Judaism, the Background of Christianity, the Lost Library of Qumran* (New York: Doubleday, 1995), 84–97.

10. 1QS, the "Community Rule" from the Dead Sea Scrolls.

11. 1QM, the "War Rule," from the Dead Sea Scrolls.

12. Josephus, *Antiquities* 13.288-98, 372-73, 380.

13. Josephus, *Antiquities* 18.23; *War* 2.118.

14. Josephus, *Antiquities* 18.23.

15. See further Horsley, *Jesus and the Spiral of Violence,* 77-89.

16. Josephus, *War* 2.425, 433-56. Fuller discussion in Richard A. Horsley, "The Sicarii: Ancient Jewish Terrorists," *Journal of Religion* 59 (1979): 435-58.

17. Documentation and analysis in Richard A. Horsley, "Popular Messianic Movements around the Time of Jesus," *Catholic Biblical Quarterly* 46 (1984): 471-93; and "'Like One of the Prophets of Old'": Two Types of Popular Prophets at the Time of Jesus," *Catholic Biblical Quarterly* 47 (1985): 435-63.

18. See the fuller analysis and critical discussion in Horsley, *Jesus and the Spiral of Violence*; Richard A. Horsley, *Hearing the Whole Story: The Politics of Plot in Mark's Gospel* (Louisville: Westminster John Knox, 2001); *Jesus and Empire: The Kingdom of God and the New World Disorder* (Minneapolis: Fortress Press, 2003); and Horsley and Draper, *Whoever Hears You Hears Me.*

19. Josephus, *Against Apion* 2.75-77; *War* 2.197; Philo, *On the Embassy to Gaius* 157.

20. Josephus, *War* 2.409-17.

21. So Goodman, *Ruling Class of Judea.*

22. See further Lee I. Levine, *The Rabbinic Class of Palestine in Late Antiquity* (New York: Jewish Theological Seminary of America, 1989), and Shaye J. D. Cohen, "The Place of the Rabbi in Jewish Society of the

Second Century," in *The Galilee in Late Antiquity,* ed.
Lee I. Levine (New York: Jewish Theological Seminary
of America, 1992), 157–73.

Chapter 5

1. Edward N. Luttwak, *The Grand Strategy of the
Roman Empire from the First Century A.D. to the Third*
(Baltimore: Johns Hopkins Univ. Press, 1976).

2. Michel Foucault, *Power/Knowledge: Selected In-
terviews and Other Writings, 1927–1977,* ed. and
trans. Colin Gordon (New York: Pantheon, 1980).

3. The following sketch depends heavily on Simon
Price, *Rituals and Power: The Roman Imperial Cult in
Asia Minor* (Cambridge: Cambridge Univ. Press, 1984),
and Paul Zanker, *The Power of Images in the Age of Augustus,* trans. Alan Shapiro (Ann Arbor: Univ. of Michi-
gan Press, 1988). See also Steven Friesen, *Imperial
Cults and the Apocalypse of John: Reading Revelation
in the Ruins* (New York: Oxford Univ. Press, 2001). Ex-
cerpts from Price and Zanker are reprinted in Richard
A. Horsley, ed., *Paul and Empire: Religion and Power in
Roman Imperial Society* (Harrisburg: Trinity Press International, 1997).

4. On this paragraph, see Price, *Rituals and Power,*
47, 49.

5. Zanker, *The Power of Images in the Age of Augustus,* 74.

6. See further Richard Gordon, "The Veil of Power,"
in *Paul and Empire,* 134–35.

7. Price, *Rituals and Power,* 59–65; Zanker, *The
Power of Images in the Age of Augustus,* 73–74.

8. This is emphasized by Price, *Rituals and Power.*

9. Duncan Fishwick, *The Imperial Cult in the Latin West: Studies in the Ruler Cult of the Western Provinces of the Roman Empire,* vol. 1 (Leiden: Brill, 1987).

Chapter 6

1. Stephen Nissenbaum, *The Battle for Christmas* (New York: Knopf, 1996); James Tracy, "The Armistice over Christmas: Consuming in the Twentieth Century," in *Christmas Unwrapped: Consumerism, Christ, and Culture,* ed. Richard Horsley and James Tracy (Harrisburg: Trinity Press International, 2001), 9–18.

2. Max A. Myers, "Santa Claus as an Icon of Grace," in *Christmas Unwrapped,* 188–98.

3. Richard A. Horsley, "Christmas: The Religion of Consumer Capitalism," in *Christmas Unwrapped,* 165–87.

4. Ibid.

5. Fuller analysis in Paula M. Cooey, "What Child *Is* This? *Lynch v. Donnelly* and the Celebration of Christmas in the United States," in *Christmas Unwrapped,* 199–218.

6. Kathleen Sands, "Still Dreaming: War, Memory, and Nostalgia in the American Christmas," in *Christmas Unwrapped,* 58–59.

7. Ibid., 58.

8. Ibid.

9. Horsley, "Christmas."

10. Sands, "Still Dreaming," and Max A. Myers, "Christmas on Celluloid: Hollywood Helps Construct the American Christmas," in *Christmas Unwrapped,* 39–54.

11. David R. Loy, "The Religion of the Market," *Journal of the American Academy of Religion* 65 (1997): 275–90.

12. As criticized by Talal Asad, *Genealogies of Religion: Discipline and Reasons of Power in Christianity and Islam* (Baltimore: Johns Hopkins Univ. Press, 1993), 27–54.

13. Clifford Geertz, "Religion as a Cultural System," in *The Interpretation of Cultures: Selected Essays* (New York: Basic, 1973), 89–126.

14. The following discussion and quotations are from Asad, *Genealogies of Religion,* 46.

15. Arthur P. Simonds, "The Holy Days and the Wholly Dazed," in *Christmas Unwrapped,* 84–109.

16. Ibid.

17. Ibid.

18. Horsley, "Christmas."

19. On the deep biblical and other religious streams in American history, culture, and self-identity, see especially Robert N. Bellah, *The Broken Covenant: American Civil Religion in a Time of Trial* (Chicago: Univ. of Chicago Press, 1992). On political-religious American sense of manifest destiny, see especially the concise recent analysis and presentation in Anders Stephanson, *Manifest Destiny: American Expansion and the Empire of Right* (New York: Hill and Wang, 1995).

Epilogue

1. Carleton J. H. Hayes, *Nationalism: A Religion* (New York: Macmillan, 1960), and Mark Juergensmeyer, *The New Cold War? Religious Nationalism Confronts the Secular State* (Berkeley: Univ. of California Press, 1993).